NARROW GAUGE LINES OF THE BRITISH ISLES

NARROW GAUGE LINES OF THE BRITISH ISLES

PETER JOHNSON

Ian Allan PUBLISHING

Contents

First published 2015

ISBN 978 0 7110 3766 3

© Peter Johnson 2015

Published by Ian Allan Publishing Ltd, Hersham, Surrey KT12 4RG.

Printed in China.

Visit the Ian Allan Publishing website at www.ianallanpublishing.com

FRONT COVER With a dusting of snow on the Moelwyns, the Festiniog Railway's Hunslet 2-4-0STT *Blanche* shunts out onto the Glaslyn embankment at Porthmadog on 29 March 2009. *Author*

BACK COVER A classic scene on the Lynton & Barnstaple Railway, but a few weeks later the railway would be closed. *The Times*

PREVIOUS PAGE In 1865 the Festiniog Railway became the first narrow gauge railway to carry passengers. Fairlie *Merddin Emrys*, built in the railway's own works in 1879, and a train of restored and recreated 19th century carriages stand at Tan y Bwlch on 20 April 2011. *Author*

ABOVE There were several narrow gauge electric tramways, including the Llandudno & Colwyn Bay Electric Railway, a 3ft 6in gauge line eight miles long which opened in 1907 and closed in 1956. Had it lasted another 10 years or so it might have survived as a popular tourist attraction. The photograph shows the scene at Penrhyn Hill circa 1907.

Introduction

JAMES SPOONER WAS RESPONSIBLE for the Festiniog Railway's survey and the alignment that gave it the manageable gradient between the Blaenau Ffestiniog slate quarries and Portmadoc harbour, enabling loaded trains to be run by gravity. His son, Charles Easton Spooner, was responsible for developing the FR after his father died, converting it to steam traction and introducing passenger services. He was also responsible for the 1871 survey of the North Wales Narrow Gauge Railways and for that used in the reconstruction of the Penrhyn Railway in 1876.

One of his successors at the NWNGR was James Cleminson, said to be an associate of Robert Fairlie, who designed a form of articulation for six-wheeled vehicles that was used on NWNGR rolling stock and on the 3-foot-gauge Manx Northern and Southwold Railways. Cleminson's successor at the NWNGR was Robert H. Livesey, who left Wales to manage the Finn Valley Railway and then the County Donegal Railway in Ireland.

In turn, Livesey's successor as NWNGR engineer was James W. Szlumper, who became engineer of the Vale of Rheidol Railway and the Lynton & Barnstaple Railway.

Earlier, James Swinton Spooner, another of James Spooner's sons, had been the Talyllyn Railway's engineer, and Thomas John Spooner, one of his grandsons, had worked on the Darjeeling Himalayan Railway, where he might have influenced the design of some of that railway's four-wheeled carriages that had some resemblance to FR quarrymen's carriages. Charles Edwin Spooner, one of Charles's sons, was resident engineer on the NWNGR between 1874 and 1876 and later became the first general manager and chief engineer of the Federated Malay States Railways.

These links serve to show how railways of different gauges and in different locations may be connected in ways that belie their appearance.

Since the 2ft 3in-gauge Talyllyn Railway became the first preserved railway in 1951, narrow gauge railways have played a significant role in the development of what has become known as the heritage railway movement, becoming major players in the tourism industry. They range from short lines in parks to the newly revived 25-mile-long Welsh Highland Railway.

Narrow gauge railways were first used in industry, particularly in quarries and mines where using a narrower-than-standard track gauge enabled wagons to be pushed by men or pulled by animals. The narrow tracks could negotiate sharper curves and access more difficult locations, and required simpler, cheaper earthworks because they could more easily follow the contours. Because the lines were invariably isolated there was very little standardisation in the gauge adopted.

In Britain the greatest use of narrow gauge railways was, and remains, concentrated in North Wales, where large volumes of slate in mountainous terrain and the need to contain costs were especially important, the result being a wide variety of lines coincidentally built in scenic locations, which turned out to be essential to the continued existence of many of them.

The earliest here were tramways serving collieries and ironstone workings in the Dee valley around Wrexham, late in the 18th century.

They were followed by the Penrhyn Railway in Caernarfonshire, a slate railway built between 1876 and 1879 incorporating routes dating back to 1798 and 1801. Nearby, the Dinorwic quarries' use of tramways was first recorded in 1813. An 1824 2-foot-gauge line connecting them to Port Dinorwic was superseded by the 4-foot-gauge Padarn Railway on a different alignment in 1843. Both the Penrhyn system and Dinorwic's internal lines used the 1ft 10¾in gauge. These systems were built on the quarry-owners' own land and required no powers.

To the south-west, the Nantlle quarry owners faced a different situation when they wished to improve the transport of their slate to the harbour at Caernarfon. They combined to obtain an Act of Parliament in 1825 and opened their 3ft 6in-gauge railway in 1828. Traffic on these lines was horse-powered, and none of them officially carried passengers.

To the south, the Festiniog Railway's main traffic ran by gravity, with horses pulling empty wagons, and some back traffic, up to the quarries. The 1ft 11½in-gauge railway was authorised by an 1832 Act of Parliament and opened in 1836; it is convenient to refer to the gauge as 2 feet.

Despite the promise of cheaper rates, initially only one of the Ffestiniog quarry owners supported it. Once the others had overcome their reluctance to use the railway, it became profitable and started paying dividends to its shareholders. In 1863 George England supplied it with the first three of six steam locomotives. They were not the first narrow gauge steam engines; the credit for that goes to the Coalbrookdale Company for building a 3-foot-gauge Trevithick-type locomotive in 1803. The FR was not the first British narrow gauge steam railway, either; the credit for that lies with the 4-foot-gauge Redruth & Chasewater Railway, which had started services in 1825/26, carrying copper ore and coal; it used steam locomotives from 1854 and closed in 1915, never having carried passengers.

The conflict between the standard gauge and Brunel's 7ft 0¼in broad gauge caused Parliament to enact the Gauge of Railways Act in 1846, forbidding the construction of any public railway to a gauge other than standard. The legislators did not envisage a situation arising where an existing authorised railway of a non-standard gauge might be adapted to carry passengers.

The Festiniog Railway's acquisition of its first steam engines was soon followed by suitable rolling stock, and passenger services were started on 5 January 1865. The FR's gauge was the narrowest used on a British public railway, however, until the Ravenglass & Eskdale Railway was converted from a 3-foot to a 15-inch gauge, without approval, in 1915. The FR's usage set the precedent for the use of narrow gauge more widely, both in Britain and overseas.

This came about after the government inspector Captain Henry Whatley Tyler presented a paper entitled 'On the Festiniog Railway for Passengers: as a 2-feet gauge, with sharp curves, and worked by locomotive engines' to members of the Institution of Civil Engineers on 11 April 1865. He described the FR's background and explained what made it significant. It had been built cheaply, although increasing traffic had required the alignment and track to be improved. The load was taken to the port by gravity. The introduction of steam traction had been a success and permitted the carriage of passengers.

He observed that many parts of Britain had benefited from the introduction of railways, but that there were other areas that would benefit while not justifying the costs incurred in constructing standard gauge railways. Standard gauge lines could be built more cheaply if they had steeper gradients, but to work them would require heavier engines that would require more substantial bridges and stronger permanent way, increasing construction costs.

In some areas the use of a narrower gauge, with the concomitant use of lighter track materials, less ballast, cheaper earthworks with sharper curves and lighter locomotives and rolling stock, could do all the work required, especially where high speed was not required and the traffic was not heavy.

The Norwegian government, he commented, had built two 3ft 6in-gauge lines that operated at average speeds of 15mph and were so satisfactory that another line was being built and there was no intention of using any other gauge. In Queensland, Australia, 100 miles of 3ft 6in-gauge was being built and more was being planned.

However, in Britain development of sub-standard gauges was hampered by the 1846 Gauge Act already mentioned. Recommended in a report of the Gauge Commissioners, who had a strong feeling against 'break of gauge' between different railways and the inconvenience it caused with transhipment, the Act forbade the construction of any railway intended for the carriage of passengers to less than standard gauge in Great Britain and less than 5ft 3in in Ireland. The Act did not affect existing railways. There was not then, Tyler observed, any prospect of a narrower gauge being extensively required.

However, there was now, he declared, an increasing demand for branch railways of a 'minor class'. Mineral lines used a narrower gauge and some were being constructed with the carriage of passengers in mind. Therefore the 1846 Act should be repealed or its provisions modified. While there should not be any change of gauge on trunk routes, this was less significant with feeder branches where the use of standard gauge could not be commercially practicable. Passengers had to change trains in any event and it was much cheaper to tranship goods from one railway truck to another than to cart them for several miles over indifferent roads.

The Festiniog was an extreme example, he said, maintaining its original gauge because of the restrictions imposed by its original works and those of the tramways and inclines that connected to it. It was outdone by the 18-inch-gauge railway at the London & North Western Railway's Crewe locomotive works, but the cost of that railway could not be taken as a guide for the future.

Now Tyler thought that a gauge wider than 2ft would be desirable for any new line and it would not be worthwhile diverting from standard gauge for anything other than 2ft 6in. Such lines would cost two-thirds the cost of standard gauge branches and could be worked and maintained for three-quarters of the equivalent cost. They would be of decided benefit to Great Britain and Ireland and in the Colonies, 'in fact wherever there are people to travel, produce to be transported, or resources to be developed, where it would not be commercially profitable to incur the expense, in the first instance, of a first-class railway.'

In one sense, he thought the question of gauge was one of speed. Travelling on 2-foot-gauge with 2-foot driving wheels might be made as safe as travelling on the Great Western Railway's 7-foot gauge with 7-foot driving wheels at 70mph. On the Festiniog Railway he had felt quite safe travelling at 30mph.

Tyler's audience included some of the most prominent engineers of the day and the discussion that followed continued over two evenings. Comments and observations made were both varied and wide-ranging.

George Willoughby Hemans, a Welsh engineer responsible for many early Irish lines on the 5ft 3in gauge, said that he had been asked to determine the suitability of extending a proposed competitor to the FR into the quarries at standard gauge and had concluded that it would be impracticable to do so; no better thing could be devised than the existing 2-foot gauge. If the standard gauge branch was built as far as the foot of the inclines and the narrow gauge wagons collected there, it would be a great inconvenience to transfer them onto standard gauge transporter wagons for haulage to the port. Therefore he supported the use of steam locomotives on the 2-foot gauge between the port and the inclines.

Sir Charles Fox, the engineer knighted for his part in building the 'Crystal Palace' for the 1851 Great Exhibition, developed his theory that locomotive axle loads should be no greater than the greatest wagon axle load. For 5ft 6in-gauge lines in India, 6 tons was the optimum loading and could be carried on 35lb rail. Regardless of whether the gauge was 3ft 6in, 4ft 6in or 5ft 6in, rolling stock need not be proportionately heavier in relation to the greater width of the gauge. He expected the Indian government to adhere to its resolution that branch lines should be the same gauge as the main lines, but managers complained that they had no proper control over their servants and that if a man was accustomed to drive an engine of 30 tons on the main line, he could, if he chose, run the same engine on to the lighter branch line, very much to its injury, whereas having a different gauge effectually prevented this being done.

If asked to establish an international gauge he would choose 5ft 4in, although the Irish 5ft 3in was good. The Indian 5ft 6in required rather heavy rolling stock, he thought. In his opinion 4ft 8½in was too narrow. Unless there was a good reason for diverting from what he called a country's universal gauge, he would use it even on light feeder lines.

Several members thought that considerable economy in the earthworks arose by adopting sharp and reverse curves, although some structures were no cheaper. With the narrow gauge, a shorter engine wheelbase could be adopted to make traversing sharp curves easier.

George Parker Bidder, who had worked with Robert Stephenson on the London & Birmingham Railway and a former President of the ICE,

LEFT One of the few 2ft 3in gauge railways, the Plynlimon & Hafan Tramway was opened in 1897 and closed at the end of 1898. Some of its assets, including the Bagnall 2-4-0T *Talybont* were regauged and found new lives in the construction and operating of the Vale of Rheidol Light Railway (pages 34 and 56).

ABOVE Less than 2 miles long, the 3-foot-gauge Rye & Camber Tramway was opened between Rye and Rye golf course in 1895, being extended to Camber Sands in 1908. The line was equipped with two Bagnall 2-4-0Ts and two carriages, and here *Victoria* waits for passengers at Rye on 10 April 1909. Bagnall also built the larger carriage; the balconies were enclosed at a later date. The smaller carriage had been built locally in 1896, at the Rother Ironworks in Rye, for the use of 3rd Class passengers. A petrol locomotive was used from 1925. Closed on the outbreak of war in 1939, the line was scrapped in 1947. *H. L. Hopwood*

noted that the significance of Tyler's paper was that he was a government official expressing an opinion on the commercial outcomes of railway development. The narrow gauge system was not propounded as a measure of economy other than where it should be considered for the sake of the curves and gradients, in districts where the broader gauge could not be introduced. That was the only ground on which the matter should be fairly considered. Tyler did not pretend that narrow gauge could be worked more cheaply than broad gauge. The question was not the cost of moving a carriage, but the cost moving a ton of minerals, or coals, or a hundred passengers. As a matter of practice, a ton of minerals, or a hundred passengers, could not be moved on the narrow gauge more cheaply than on a broader gauge.

With regard to the Festiniog Railway, Charles Hutton Gregory, the vice president, thought the circumstances were special and peculiar but that the Institution and the profession would be bold if they adopted the concept of using narrow gauge on small branch lines in circumstances like the FR, where it would have been exceedingly difficult to adopt standard gauge. The FR had made the most of what it had in making the line suitable for general goods and passengers. It had also done well to introduce locomotives. He objected to the theory that working expenses were proportionate to the cube of a railway's gauge – the volume of goods and the number of passengers were also relevant. He was sure that George England would agree that, although had got his engines to work under difficult circumstances and with an exceptionally narrow gauge, locomotives built for wider gauges would be both more powerful and more economical.

Gregory thought that the savings in construction costs would have been minimal. The minimum width was 11 feet for single track and 20 feet for double, compared with 12ft 8in and 23ft 5in respectively on standard gauge. Because rolling stock was built with rigid parallel axles, the narrow gauge was able to adopt curves of smaller radii, in this respect giving it an advantage over standard gauge. However, the advent of radial axles would enable standard gauge lines to accommodate sharper curves in the future.

Thomas Elliott Harrison, the North Eastern Railway's engineer, said that if the FR had been a standard gauge line then the slate would

have been transhipped at the foot of the inclines and again into ships at the harbour. But it was not, so the narrow gauge was unquestionably the best means of conveying the traffic.

As to the carriage of passengers, no doubt it was ingenious and people travelled in comfort, but the works were so narrow that when the train was standing in a cutting a passenger could hardly make his way past the carriages. This was not to be taken as a sample of what was desirable. It was a clever adaptation of a state of things that previously existed, and which had been designed with a different object, and as far as it went it was exceedingly good; but to suppose that the principle upon which it was constructed was to be applied to an unlimited extent where standard gauge railways existed was a total fallacy.

On the other hand, the Midland Railway's general manager, James Joseph Allport, objected to the widespread use of narrow gauge feeder lines. Locomotives could be constructed to handle the same loads as on the standard gauge but at the expense of increased wear and tear. The greatest problem, however, was transhipment, particularly the movement of heavier wagons. If the narrow gauge was to be adopted it should only be as branches to main lines, albeit at the additional capital cost of additional land at junctions and in the construction of special rolling stock.

James Brunlees, who declared that he had been the engineer of the 3-foot-gauge tramway built to serve the Gorsedda slate quarry, eight miles from Portmadoc, in 1856, said that he knew the FR well; he did not question the mechanical success of its locomotives but doubted the railway's commercial viability. Although he had recommended the use of the narrow gauge for the Gorsedda line, he would only recommend its further use in exceptional circumstances.

Peter William Barlow, the engineer responsible for several railways and the Tower Subway, was not convinced that a 2-foot gauge, or anything near it, could serve any useful purpose, but recognised that it was inconceivable for one gauge to suit all circumstances. It was the width of carriages that had the biggest influence on construction costs, not gauge. He noted Tyler's report that the Festiniog locomotives weighing 7½ tons could take 50 tons up gradients of 1 in 60, and contrasted it with the Metropolitan Railway, where engines weighing 40 tons were used on lighter loads, adding that the Metropolitan operated a frequent service with light trains that needed quick acceleration.

In contrast, William Robert Galbraith, then engaged on building the Thames bridge at Kew, made the case for standard gauge light railways to serve sparsely populated agricultural districts.

George England, the locomotive builder, brought the discussion to an end by saying that the FR's gauge should not be considered a pattern for universal adoption. As built, locomotive working had not been contemplated. Using horses, the owners had been satisfied by the traction and the dividends earned. The adoption of locomotives had been a defence against competition from a proposed standard gauge line, the Aberystwyth & Welsh Coast Railway's Festiniog branch. He had been required to produce locomotives capable of hauling 25 tons up a gradient of 1 in 60 at 6mph; the first had managed 50 tons at 12mph. The ruling gradient being closer to 1 in 80 than 1 in 60 would account for some of that performance increase, however.

Later in 1865 Charles Easton Spooner, the Festiniog Railway's secretary and engineer, who oversaw the line's adaptation to locomotive haulage, presented a paper at the Inventors' Institute; he had not been present when Tyler had spoken at the ICE. Setting out the case for narrow gauge and describing the FR, he concluded that 2ft 6in or 2ft 9in would be the most suitable sub-standard gauge. The increased width would allow the boiler to be made larger and mounted higher to improve access for maintenance. His proposal for flangeless trailing wheels to steady the ride was overtaken by the adoption of Robert Fairlie's articulated locomotive in 1869.

The ICE thought sufficiently well of Tyler's paper to award him a Telford medal and premium for it in August 1865. The Institute's members did not take up the challenge of developing narrow gauge branch lines, however. It took the delivery of a new Festiniog Railway locomotive to elevate the cause of the narrow gauge and the FR in particular into the international arena.

The FR at that time was under pressure from the Festiniog quarry owners to provide the capacity needed to carry increasing volumes of slate, much in demand because of industrial development in Britain and overseas. From 64,000 tons in 1862, more than 90,000 tons had been carried in 1868. Not understanding how its passing places could be developed to increase capacity, the FR had obtained powers to rebuild the railway with double track. While the Parliamentary process was under way an order was placed for a Fairlie articulated locomotive, delivered within a few weeks of the FR's bill receiving the Royal Assent.

With two four-wheel power bogies and a double boiler, the new locomotive was named *Little Wonder* and was soon found to be capable of hauling loads of 140 tons over the entire line at 15mph, nearly three times the load and at a greater speed than the original locomotives. No wonder the FR soon suspended its plans to build a second track. *Little Wonder*'s achievements, and more, were brought to the attention of the wider world in a two-part article published in *The Engineer* in September and October 1869. The magazine particularly noticed that the rolling stock had been adapted to the traffic and very

little dead weight was being carried when compared with standard gauge lines. It also drew attention to the profits made and the dividends paid to shareholders.

Maybe because of these articles, Tsar Alexander was persuaded that the 'Fairlie system', 2ft 6in gauge with double locomotives, could be adopted to open Russia to development. Fairlie visited St Petersburg to explain the benefits and a commission was appointed to investigate. Arrangements were made for the commission to visit the Festiniog Railway, and to see a Fairlie locomotive in action on the standard gauge Brecon & Merthyr Railway.

Over two days the capabilities of *Little Wonder* were demonstrated, and contrasted with those of four-coupled locomotives, to a party that exceeded 40 in number, including engineers from the India Office, France, Sweden, Norway, Switzerland and Germany, and engineers and managers from other British railways as well as the Russian dignitaries. The event was chaired by the Duke of Sutherland and Tyler acted as secretary, keeping a record of events. It was widely reported.

An unexpected consequence for the FR was that Tyler, noting the changes and improvements made to the railway since his 1864 visit, recommended to the Board of Trade that the railway be released from its obligation, imposed by him, to restrict train speeds to 10-12mph. The track was much improved and the company had demonstrated its ability to carry passengers safely, he explained.

The news reports did much to promote the use of the narrow gauge internationally and boosted the Festiniog Railway's reputation enormously. There was a steady stream of visitors to Portmadoc, and whenever a proposal was made for a narrow gauge railway to be built in Britain its description invariably included the phrase 'like the Festiniog Railway'. Mostly, though, the effect of the demonstrations was felt overseas.

Not everyone was taken in by the FR's promotion as a solution for the role of railways in opening up remote areas. One such was Guilford L. Molesworth, the director of public works for Ceylon, who in 1871 compiled a report for the Government of Victoria, Australia. Already a sceptic in the cause of light railways, he found that the FR's case had been underestimated or misrepresented and that it benefited from being able to charge higher rates for the slate traffic than standard gauge railways normally charged for minerals. The sharper curves cited as a benefit of the narrow gauge, he claimed, could equally be adopted on standard gauge lines provided lower speeds were used.

The Russians, however, had submitted a positive report on their observations, and in June 1871 Spooner was presented with a gold medal signifying the Tsar's 'recognition of his [Spooner's] cordial reception of the Imperial Commission'. Fairlie's obituary in *The Times* on 3 August 1885 said that he had been presented with a medal as well, but this seems not to have been reported at the time.

It might also be mentioned that in Britain there was much interest in what the French called 'secondary railways' since Section V of the 1868 Regulation of Railways Act allowed the Board of Trade to licence light railways. Of the few railways that took advantage of this, the Southwold and Ravenglass & Eskdale Railways and the Vale of Rheidol Light Railway were narrow gauge, although the latter had been brought within the remit of the 1896 Light Railways Act by the time it opened in 1902.

While attention was focused on the Festiniog Railway's use of steam locomotives, in 1865 the Talyllyn Railway had become the first non-standard-gauge railway to receive Parliamentary approval for the carriage of passengers since the Gauge of Railways Act. It used the 2ft 3in gauge, the same used by the nearby Corris Railway, a horse- and gravity-worked mineral railway opened in 1859 serving quarries working the same slate vein as those served by the TR at Bryn Eglwys.

Despite having a wider track gauge, these railways' loading gauge was much smaller than that of most 2-foot-gauge lines.

Only two other public railways were to use the 2ft 3in gauge, the short-lived Plynlimon & Hafan Tramway in Cardiganshire, which was opened in 1897, and the Campbeltown & Macrihanish Light Railway on the Mull of Kintyre in Scotland, opened in 1906.

Two railways on the Wales-England border near Shrewsbury used the very similar 2ft 4½in gauge. In Denbighshire, the Glyn Valley Tramway was a roadside horse tramway opened in 1873, while in Shropshire the Snailbeach District Railways was a mineral line that never carried passengers, opening in 1877.

On the 2-foot gauge, the Festiniog & Blaenau Railway was opened in 1868, an independent feeder to the FR, although it had a short life in this form, being acquired by the Great Western Railway and converted to standard gauge in 1883.

Further north, in Caernarfonshire, the North Wales Narrow Gauge Railways was opened in stages between 1877 and 1881, two routes primarily serving slate quarries, one of them terminating at the foot of Snowdon. With the FR's secretary and engineer, Charles E. Spooner, as its engineer, its use of the same gauge was perhaps not so surprising. It never fully overcame the financial problems that engulfed it before it was opened.

Possibly the ultimate development on this gauge was the Lynton & Barnstaple Railway, with a route nearly 20 miles long across Exmoor, which opened in 1898. Its engineer was James W. Szlumper, who had held that position on the NWNGR since 1891. Unlike most others, it was well equipped.

In Britain, the enthusiasm shown for the narrow gauge in the 1870s had been mostly manifest in Ireland, where several 3-foot-gauge lines were developed from 1872 onwards. Some of them were quite extensive and used large locomotives. Ireland was also, of course, the home of the distinctive Listowel & Ballybunion Railway, a Lartigue monorail, arguably a railway with no gauge at all. From 1874 most railways in the Isle of Man were also of 3-foot-gauge. In England the only 3-foot-gauge public passenger lines were the Ravenglass & Eskdale Railway (1876) and the Southwold Railway (1879). In industry, several companies also used the 3-foot gauge, notably the

ABOVE Sir Arthur Heywood's development of 15 inches as a practical gauge was far more influential than he could have imagined, finding extensive use in tourism. Seen circa 1910, 0-6-0T *Shelagh* was one of three locomotives that he built for his only customer, the Duke of Westminster. It was scrapped in 1942.

British Aluminium Corporation's Lochaber Railway near Fort William, which had a 19-mile-long main line, and some East Midlands iron ore quarries.

Until the 1960s and the widespread availability of suitable motor vehicles, contractors often used temporary narrow gauge railways. Tunnelling projects still do, 3-foot-gauge lines being used in the construction of the Channel Tunnel and 2ft 6in or 3 feet on London's Crossrail contracts.

While most industrial lines used a 2-foot gauge or thereabouts, the British Insulated Callender's Cable Company's Erith works used a 3ft 6in gauge and the Waltham iron ore quarry in Leicestershire used a metre gauge. The most unusual gauge of 3ft 2¼in was used by the Dorking Greystone Lime Company in Surrey.

Largely because of the Board of Trade's reluctance to accept a reduction in standards on lightly used lines, few railways took advantage of the 1868 Regulation of Railways Act's provisions for light railways, the cost of obtaining powers also inhibiting development. Section V of the 1868 Act was replaced by the Light Railways Act in 1896, which resulted in a brief upsurge in British narrow gauge development, in two phases. The Act permitted the authorisation of railways by means of quasi-Parliamentary Light Railway Orders made by the Light Railway Commission and confirmed by the Board of Trade.

Several narrow gauge lines were built as light railways and others were 'downgraded' to take advantage of the benefits offered, including financial support from local authorities. The Act was responsible for two 2ft 6in-gauge railways, as recommended in the 1870s, the Leek & Manifold Railway and the Welshpool & Llanfair Light Railway. The former was the first narrow gauge light railway authorised, although the second was the first built. Both were operated by standard gauge railway companies to qualify them for local authority and Treasury loans and grants.

During the First World War the trenches were generally served by 2-foot-gauge railways that mostly used British or American equipment. Later, 2ft 6in gauge was taken up by the military for use in various depots.

The final flowering of 'traditional' 2-foot-gauge lines arrived in the 1920s, with the Welsh Highland Railway and the Ashover Light Railway. The first was a local authority-led scheme that combined the then moribund North Wales Narrow Gauge Railways with the abandoned and incomplete Portmadoc, Beddgelert & South Snowdon Railway to make a 22-mile route between Dinas, 3 miles from Caernarfon, and Porthmadog, which opened throughout in 1923.

The Ashover Light Railway was a development of the Clay Cross Company in Derbyshire. Opened in 1925, it had Colonel H. F. Stephens as its engineer. Known for his involvement with a collection of cash-strapped light railways, Stephens was also involved with the Festiniog and Welsh Highland lines in the 1920s.

Earlier, the 18-inch-gauge Sand Hutton Light Railway in Yorkshire had opened in 1922, superseding an earlier 15-inch-gauge line built for the owner's amusement. The wider gauge was chosen to take advantage of cheaply available war-surplus railway equipment.

Narrow gauge railways in scenic locations were instantly attractive to tourists. Although targeted at residents, the earliest recorded excursion on the Festiniog railway took place on Easter Monday 1865, just four months after the passenger service had started. The earliest reference linking that railway to tourism had been made in 1842, on the occasion of the opening of the long tunnel. It was not long, in any event, before the small equipment of the FR and other narrow gauge lines earned them the appellation 'toy railways', and the carriage of tourists became a vital part of their traffic. Sooner or later narrow gauge railways would be built with tourists as their main purpose.

With the exception of the Welshpool & Llanfair Light Railway, which was operated by the Cambrian Railways, tourism soon became a vital component of these railways' traffic, so it is no surprise that railways were built for tourists. It is debatable whether Volk's Electric Railway, of 2-foot gauge and opened in Brighton in 1883, was a

ABOVE On the south bank of the Mawddach estuary, Fairbourne had been developed as a holiday resort by Arthur McDougall, a businessman who had made his money from milling flour. A tramway, which dated from 1896, was installed to carry bricks to building sites along Beach Road. When the development phase was ended the tramway was extended 2 miles to Penrhyn Point, opposite Barmouth, providing a link with a ferry and the Cambrian Railways station that was opened in 1899. It had no statutory authority. Two light four-wheeled open tramcars provided the passenger accommodation.

Converted to 15-inch gauge by Narrow Gauge Railways Ltd in 1916, the railway was operated as the Fairbourne Miniature Railway until 1986, when its conversion to 12¼-inch gauge was completed following a change of ownership.

The first 15-inch-gauge locomotive used on the line was Bassett-Lowke 4-4-2 *Prince Edward of Wales*, seen here in 1919. In the background one of the lesser known viaducts on the Cambrian Railways' coast line is to be seen; the timber structure was renewed in concrete by the Great Western Railway. *D. George*

demonstration of the power of electricity that happened to be a railway in a seaside resort, or vice versa. Two narrow gauge steam railways opened for tourists in the 1890s were also built on private land without Parliamentary powers, the Rye & Camber Tramway in Sussex in 1895, of 3-foot gauge, and the Snowdon Mountain Tramroad in 1896, of 800mm gauge.

The first 20th-century developments in tourist railways were influenced by the efforts of Sir Arthur Heywood Bt to determine the minimum gauge for useful railways. Concluding that it was 15 inches, he had built and equipped a demonstration line at his home at Duffield Bank, Derbyshire, from 1874. During his lifetime he had only persuaded the Duke of Westminster to adopt his principles, with a line about 3 miles long being built on the Duke's Eaton Hall estate near Chester from 1895.

The Northampton-based model maker W. J. Bassett-Lowke, and the engineer Henry Greenly, advanced the development of the 15-inch gauge for passenger railways from 1904, producing a 4-4-2 that was trialled on the Eaton Railway. More locomotives were built for temporary lines at exhibitions until the first permanent line was built around the marine lake at Rhyl in 1911.

With friends, they acquired control of the moribund Ravenglass & Eskdale Railway, re-gauging it and reopening it in 1915/16. The same group moved on to Fairbourne, on the Merionethshire coast, where flour magnate Arthur McDougall had started to develop a resort in the 1890s. The contractor's 2-foot-gauge horse-worked tramway had remained in situ and found a use carrying visitors to Penrhyn Point, on the southern bank of the Mawddach, opposite Barmouth. The tramway was re-gauged to 15 inches and steam-hauled services started in 1916. Wartime was a very busy period for these railway entrepreneurs.

The use of the 15-inch gauge was taken to the ultimate with the Romney, Hythe & Dymchurch Railway, opened between New Romney and Hythe in 1927 and extended to Dungeness the following year. Henry Greenly designed the railway and its equipment for its promoter, Captain Jack Howey. Unlike most other lines of this gauge, the RHDR was a statutory light railway, a status later shared with the Kirklees Light Railway in Yorkshire, and the Bure Valley Railway and 10¼-inch-gauge Wells & Walsingham Railway, both in Norfolk.

From 1928 several parks decided that their facilities would be enhanced by the provision of a narrow gauge railway. The locomotive builders Baguley and Hudswell, Clarke developed distinctive steam-outline internal combustion locomotives for this market, building in gauges of 1ft 8in and 2 feet. After the war other builders and several other gauges entered this arena.

Success with the preservation of the Talyllyn Railway and the revival of the Festiniog from the 1950s introduced an era of narrow gauge railways as tourist attractions. Some were enthusiast-led, some were pure commercial enterprises, and some were the result of local authority initiatives. Locations were many and varied – old industrial sites, former standard gauge trackbeds, parks, farms, quarries and otherwise private gardens.

Most industrial narrow gauge lines were closed completely as their industries expired or road haulage became more convenient. Thus, several railways were established using the obsolete assets.

The flooding of a part of the Festiniog Railway's route at Tanygrisiau by the Central Electricity Generating Board, in the course of building a pumped-storage power station, and the construction of a 2½-mile deviation, proved to be great challenge to the railway deemed impossible by many. The 13-year project, completed in 1977, was also the source of inspiration to those involved with other steam railways, showing that with determination they could be taken seriously by local and central government and that seemingly impossible ambitions could be attained.

This was certainly the case with the Welsh Highland Railway, also restored by the Festiniog Railway Company. Out of use since 1936, scrapped in 1941 and abandoned in a legal quagmire, when the first train ran between Caernarfon and Porthmadog in 2010 it was nearly 50 years since its restoration had first been mooted. The likelihood of a railway being restored through a national park on such a scale had seemed impossible for so long. Now, like other narrow gauge railways operating in the 21st century, it is making an essential contribution to the economic vitality of the area through which it runs.

Lack of space precludes the inclusion of all narrow gauge railways and in-depth descriptions of those that are included. Emphasis is given to those established by statute, while giving an impression of the uses of narrow gauge railways in industry and tourism, particularly in the use of steam locomotives.

Acknowledgements

In 1963 news of the construction of a narrow gauge railway in the garden at Cadeby Rectory circulated widely in Leicestershire as well as amongst the enthusiast fraternity. Participating in a church visit, I therefore made my first visit to a narrow gauge railway in either 1963 or 1964. My interest was not seriously piqued by the narrow gauge, however, until I became acquainted with the revived narrow gauge railways in Wales in the early 1970s. The rest, as has sometimes been said, is history.

Once again, I have the opportunity of sharing my interest in narrow gauge railways with a wider public. Returning to the album format after more than 10 years has been an interesting and challenging exercise, taking more time than expected. Photographers are acknowledged where known, but unfortunately many of the photographs bought via the internet are sold in ignorance of their origins. The historical photographs are from the publisher's and my own collection. The postcards are from my collection.

Many thanks to Michael Farr who several years ago gave me his Manx negatives and transparencies. And many thanks, too, to all those at the railways still operational who have been so welcoming over the years.

Finally, many thanks to Peter Waller who for many years managed to keep me gainfully occupied while he was employed by the publisher.

Peter Johnson
Leicester
August 2014

1

Parliamentary railways

It was a requirement that railways intended for public use, particularly the carriage of passengers, needed an Act of Parliament. Such Acts essentially declared that the proposal was in the public interest and gave the promoters powers to raise capital, to borrow money and to acquire land compulsorily, as well as the powers required to build and operate their undertaking.

Narrow gauge railways empowered by Acts of Parliament were the Festiniog, Corris, Talyllyn, North Wales Narrow Gauge, Ravenglass & Eskdale, Southwold, Snailbeach District, Lynton & Barnstaple and Vale of Rheidol, and the Glyn Valley Tramway. The Portmadoc, Beddgelert & South Snowdon Railway, which became part of the Welsh Highland Railway, included two Acts in its legislative portfolio.

❧

The role the **Festiniog Railway** played in influencing the development of narrow gauge railways around the world was touched on in the introduction. As it translated from its origins as a horse- and gravity-

worked mineral railway to being a locomotive-worked general carrier, its profitability attracted international attention, inspiring the construction of other narrow gauge railways, some adopting the same gauge, some adopting a wider gauge.

The Festiniog Railway Act was obtained in 1832, authorising the construction and operation of a route surveyed by James Spooner the previous year. The name was taken from the parish in which the line started.

The incentive to build a railway was the slate quarries in the Ffestiniog area. The slate was, and remains, of good quality, but its use was constrained by the expense of transporting it by pack animals and small boats to the sea, close to the present town of Porthmadog, a distance of about 14 miles. There it was transhipped to coastal craft. These transfers also damaged the slate, requiring more to be shipped than was paid for. Not so far away, the Penrhyn and Dinorwic slate quarries had been connected to sea ports by railways from 1798 and 1824 respectively, so Ffestiniog needed a railway if its slate was to be competitive.

In 1829 quarry-owner Samuel Holland met Dubliner Henry Archer and saw a man with the drive to take on a railway scheme. Archer persuaded friends in Dublin society to put up the capital and commissioned James Spooner, who had come into the area working for the Ordnance Survey, to survey the route submitted to Parliament.

Construction was started in 1833. Archer and Spooner worked together overseeing the construction but disagreed over strategy, the former wanting to build as cheaply as possible regardless of the effect

LEFT A Festiniog Railway passenger train waits to leave Portmadoc, as was, in 1893. The quarrymen's carriage, next to the locomotive, was provided in case any quarrymen needed to travel beyond their normal routine; they could not be permitted to travel in ordinary carriages at the reduced fare they paid. The vehicle also acted as an adapter between the locomotive coupling and the carriage coupling.

on the future maintenance budget. Archer won in the short term but the railway and Spooner, and Spooner's son Charles, had to deal with the consequences for many years afterwards.

The railway was opened in 1836, the 1ft 11½in gauge taken from tramways used within the quarries. Apart from a ridge of the Moelwyns, which was crossed using inclines, Spooner's route was masterly, falling from 720 feet and maintaining an even gradient until it traversed Madocks's embankment across the Glaslyn. Stylish stone embankments carried it across gullies and ravines. Loaded wagons ran downhill by gravity in trains of four, passing the weighbridge at Boston Lodge and pulled across the embankment to the harbour by horses as required. The horses pulled the wagons back up the line.

To serve the quarries there were two branches, to Dinas and Duffws. As Holland was initially the only quarry-owner prepared to use the railway, only the former was used at first. Eventually the other quarries started using the railway and before long ten private mineral branches had been connected to the upper reaches of the railway. Two years after a tunnel had been built to bypass the inclines imposed by Archer, the railway paid dividends to its shareholders.

From the 1860s the FR entered a period of expansion and development that brought it to the attention of engineers and politicians around the world. When the line opened, contemporary engineering opinion held that locomotives could not be built to such a narrow gauge, but by the 1860s advances in locomotive design made it feasible. Holland still had influence over the company and put his nephew forward as locomotive designer. George England, a locomotive builder based in south London, was the chosen contractor, delivering three 0-4-0TTs in 1863 and one more in 1864, small tank engines with coal tenders. In 1867 two slightly larger locomotives to the same basic design with saddle tanks were obtained.

The first passenger carriages were ordered from Brown, Marshalls in Birmingham in 1863 and delivered the following year, tiny low-slung four-wheeled vehicles with a low centre of gravity for fear that they might otherwise fall over. In June 1864 the Board of Trade was requested to approve the railway's use by passengers and, following an inspection and report by its inspector, Captain H. W. Tyler, services started on 1 January 1865.

In his report Tyler made several recommendations that had long-lasting effect. Bars should be fixed over the windows to protect the passengers, and the doors should be locked, to protect the carriages in

ABOVE The Festiniog & Blaenau Railway had two Manning, Wardle 0-4-2STs, No 1 *Scorcher* and No 2 *Nipper*, the latter featuring in this scene at Manod. The locomotives did not outlive the conversion of their railway to standard gauge; new in 1868, they were sent for scrap in 1883.

case they came open in restricted areas. He also suggested that the company consider the use of bogie carriages, which it did from 1872.

Even with locomotives the railway was operated at its maximum. It did not understand how it could increase capacity by using passing loops, and in 1869 it obtained powers to build a second track. However, before it could do more than acquire some of the land required, the locomotive engineer Robert Francis Fairlie offered the use of his patent articulated locomotive design. The company was quickly persuaded of its benefits and a locomotive named *Little Wonder* was delivered later in 1869 and proved to be more than capable of meeting the company's needs.

The 1869 Act of Parliament also restructured the company, holders of the original shares receiving new additional shares pro rata to compensate them for the reduction in dividend that had occurred because improvements, notably the tunnel already mentioned, the short tunnel at Garnedd and improvements to the alignment, had been financed out of revenue.

An interchange with the Cambrian Railways opened at Minffordd in 1872 had little effect on business, but the railway's monopoly in the heart of Ffestiniog was breached by the LNWR in 1881 and the GWR in 1883. All three took business from the FR and its results show that its decline started from this time. The GWR branch from Bala had, incidentally, incorporated the 3½-mile-long Festiniog & Blaenau Railway, a non-statutory extension from the FR at Dolgarrog Ddu. Opened in 1868, the FR had sometimes supplied it with motive power.

On the face of it, the FR remained successful, buying new Fairlie locomotives and adding to its fleet of bogie carriages. It had great confidence in the abilities of its Boston Lodge works, with activities ranging from building new locomotives in 1879 and 1886 to casting rail chairs, although there was a tendency for the works to do things because it could, when it was probably not cost-effective.

The FR had fraught relationships with its customers and railway neighbours. The quarry-owners thought that their rates should be reduced in preference to the shareholders receiving dividends, despite the considerable reduction from which they had benefited since the

ABOVE Opened as a gravity/horse tramway in 1836, the Festiniog Railway adopted steam traction, 0-4-0Ts with tenders, in 1863/64. Increasing traffic led to the railway obtaining powers for a second track at the same time that Robert Francis Fairlie suggested that his patented articulated locomotive might be suitable. *Little Wonder* was built at George England's works in 1869 and was so successful that it was worn out in less than 20 years. It was replaced by the second locomotive to be built in the railway's own works, *Livingston Thompson*, in 1885.

railway had opened. Collectively, they would not allow the company to set rates dependent on volume, where the larger quarries would pay less per ton. The LNWR set its rates to undercut those of the FR, and the Cambrian tended to bully it over through rates, always expecting the FR to give way when a customer wanted better terms.

From 1901 the ordinary dividend dropped to less than 2%, and there were five years before the start of the First World War when it was not paid at all. For several years in the pre-war era it had been unable to meet its obligations to the preference shareholders. On the outbreak of war the railway was placed under government control and in 1915 Boston Lodge was taken over as a munitions factory. There was little benefit to the railway in this. The government undertook to maintain profits at 1913 levels, which was not much help if there were no profits. By the time control was handed back in 1921 the company's overdraft had risen from zero to £6,445.

The company was taken over by the Welsh Highland Railway (qv) promoters in 1921, a move that saw FR stock working over a 'foreign' line for the first time since the Festiniog & Blaenau Railway had been converted to standard gauge in 1883. The FR's resources were used to build the junction railways linking the two lines and a joint station in Portmadoc. A Light Railway Order obtained in 1923 authorised these and sanctioned the FR's operation as a light railway, enabling savings to be made on signalling.

In 1934 the WHR's local authority backers decided that it should not be reopened, leading to the FR taking a 21-year lease on it. After the 1936 season the FR decided that the WHR was not sustainable and withdrew from the lease, although it took some time to resolve the legalities.

The FR had always attracted tourists and this element of its traffic became more important during the inter-war years, especially when quarrymen found the competing motorbus services more convenient. From 1930 the passenger service was 'suspended', operating only during the brief holiday season. There were no more passenger trains after war was declared in September 1939.

During the Second World War trains were run as required, but by 1946 the railway was badly run down, without funds to make it safe for passenger operation. The remaining employees were given 24 hours' notice on 2 August. The directors anticipated selling the line for scrap, which conflicted with the company's legal obligation to provide a service. Eventually they were prepared to discuss the means by which enthusiasts could take over the railway to run it with volunteer support.

It took until 1954 to find a solution, when the late Alan Pegler used money borrowed from his father to buy the majority shareholding and redeem the overdraft. Services were resumed between Porthmadog and Boston Lodge in 1955, extended to Minffordd in 1956, Penrhyn in 1957 and Tan y Bwlch, 7½ miles from Porthmadog, in 1958. While the train service was successful, there was some scepticism locally about the motives behind the revival.

During the closure, the Central Electricity Generating Board had developed plans first mooted by the North Wales Power Company, one of its predecessors, to build a hydro-electric power station with a reservoir that would flood the FR's formation between the long tunnel and Tanygrisiau. Was the revival scheme merely a device to extract compensation from a public authority?

The FR's objection and claim for reinstatement were rejected, largely because its' claimed intention to complete the railway's restoration to Blaenau Ffestiniog was unconvincing – no organisation in its position had ever undertaken such a project before. A claim for loss of profits was eventually allowed with compensation being awarded in 1971.

In the meantime volunteers had started building a deviation route in 1965. To bypass the new reservoir a route had been devised using a spiral that started at Dduallt, which became a terminus in 1968, a unique feature on a passenger railway in Britain. The deviation, which included a tunnel, concealed bridges over the power station's high-pressure pipelines, numerous culverts, two level crossings and a river bridge, was completed with the resumption of services to Tanygrisiau in 1978.

Initially the CEGB had not been cooperative but its stance changed after the Ministry of Transport made a Light Railway Order for the first part of the deviation route in 1968. A second order was made in 1975. Revenue from the record passenger numbers carried through the 1960s and '70s supplemented the compensation funds to pay for the deviation, the Wales Tourist Board made a grant towards the coast of the new tunnel, and government-funded job creation schemes provided labour for the works at the rear of the power station.

Services were restored to a new station shared with British Rail at Blaenau Ffestiniog and partially funded by the then-European Economic Community in 1982. Elsewhere, capacity had been increased by installing a passing loop at Rhiw Goch in 1975 and using locomotives and carriages acquired from elsewhere and constructed in-house, the ultimate workshop project at the time being the construction of a new double Fairlie that had been completed in 1979. With attention focused on the restoration to Blaenau Ffestiniog, in the 1980s the railway and its rolling stock did not look good. A volunteer-led project to improve the appearance of stations spread throughout the railway, enhancing it greatly.

The resumption of services to Blaenau Ffestiniog brought a welcome increase in traffic that was soon offset by a longer-term reduction as the market in cheap package holidays increased.

As well as investigating the possibility of taking on the restoration of the Welsh Highland Railway, the FR started to capitalise on its heritage, a move that led to the reinstatement of original liveries, restoration of original lineside features and the recreation of 'lost' carriages and locomotives. A new double Fairlie completed in 1992

ABOVE Seven and a half miles from Porthmadog, Tan y Bwlch station has always been popular with passengers. From the 1930s the station house was occupied by permanent way ganger Will Jones and his wife Bessie, who was encouraged to greet the passenger trains wearing her Welsh national costume and to serve refreshments. Will is running towards *Taliesin, Livingston Thompson* until 1931, while Bessie turns to watch.

had the appearance of a 19th-century locomotive, a grant contributing to its cost. A subscription scheme was devised to pay for a new single Fairlie, completed in 1999. Subscriptions also paid for the construction of a new Lynton & Barnstaple Railway Manning, Wardle 2-6-2T, which was completed in 2010.

In 1999 a Festiniog Railway Society-led initiative, supported by a Heritage Lottery Fund grant, was the building of a new carriage restoration workshop in which to restore the 1872-built bogie carriages and 25 slate wagons. Since then, all the heritage stock has been restored and several new four-wheelers have been built. New bogie carriages have been built for the FR and the WHR, Boston Lodge earning a reputation for the quality of its output, undertaking locomotive restorations and carriage construction and overhauls for outside customers.

The completion of the WHR in 2010 and the start of services to Caernarfon brought expansion to the FR's Porthmadog station, already extensively altered since 1955, to accommodate both railways in 2014.

LEFT One of the 1867 locomotives, either *Welsh Pony* or *Little Giant*, is seen at Tan y Bwlch. They were rebuilt with cabs in 1890/91 and 1887/88 respectively. Occasionally these locomotives were turned to face downhill, as shown. The distinctive 'curly roof' van was one of three that entered service in 1873-76.

LEFT Bessie Jones dealing with passengers, probably selling them picture postcards of herself.

RIGHT A gravity train passing Dduallt in the 1920s.

LEFT Empty slate wagons were returned to the quarries attached to the rear of the passenger trains. At 62 feet high, Cei Mawr ('large embankment') is believed to be the largest dry-stone structure in Europe, if not in the world.

RIGHT By 1946 the slate traffic had almost dried up, the railway was badly run down and was without resources to undertake the heavy maintenance required if passenger services were to be resumed. *Princess* was photographed at Minffordd a few days before the company decided to suspend operations. *Bernard Edmonds*

BELOW With no trains running, the track became overgrown and the goats took over. This view of the line above Garnedd Tunnel on 13 July 1956 shows every sleeper rotted through. *M. G. W. Wheeler*

BELOW The Festiniog Railway revival started with services between Portmadoc and Boston Lodge in 1955. The first trains were hauled by the Simplex tractor, subsequently named *Mary Ann*. Two weeks later 0-4-0STT *Prince* entered service. During that first year there were only two carriages available. Penrhyn was reached in 1957, after a loop had been built and a third carriage had been restored. *George Hearse*

ABOVE *Merddin Emrys* re-entered service with its 1921 boiler in 1961. The last Fairlie in service before the line closed, it had been left with water in its tanks and boiler, and damp slack in its bunkers. This combination meant that its boiler would not last too long, and it required new tanks before it was returned to work. Running round at Tan y Bwlch in June 1963, *Merddin Emrys* looks smart but was not at all reliable. In 1968 it was dismantled for a new boiler to be fitted.

BELOW The double Fairlie *Taliesin* re-entered service in 1956 with a boiler that dated from 1905, and was renamed *Earl of Merioneth* in 1961. The standard carriage livery became varnished mahogany from 1964 but it did not wear well and was replaced by plain cherry red from 1968.

RIGHT Seen at Minffordd in the 1960s, Hunslet 0-4-0ST *Linda* was obtained on loan from the Penrhyn quarry railway in 1962 and purchased together with *Blanche* the following year; they had been built in 1893. On the FR they were rebuilt as 2-4-0STs with tenders.

RIGHT 'Y Cymro' ('The Welshman') was a non-stop extra to Tan y Bwlch launched in 1963, and is seen passing Minffordd weigh house; the weighing tables on the mineral line remained in situ until 1976.

LEFT Seen arriving at Tan y Bwlch, *Mountaineer* is an Alco 2-6-2T built for War Department service in France in 1917. In 1966 it was acquired by an English enthusiast and FR Society director who thought it might be useful. He gave it to the FR in 1967. It is carrying its namesake's bell. Once it had been reboilered in 1982 it was used extensively, but has been out of service for several years.

ABOVE *Earl of Merioneth* passes Dduallt Manor. On the right is Campbell's Platform, with its siding that accommodated the owner's diesel locomotive.

BELOW Services to Blaenau Ffestiniog were resumed in 1982. The achievement required the construction of a 2½-mile deviation around the Tanygrisiau power station's lake, which had flooded the original formation. The locomotive is *Earl of Merioneth*, built at Boston Lodge around a new Hunslet boiler. It entered service in 1979 and replaced its predecessor of the same name, the erstwhile *Taliesin*, which since 1988 has been exhibited at the National Railway Museum bearing its original name, *Livingston Thompson*.

RIGHT *David Lloyd George* is the fourth double Fairlie to be built at Boston Lodge. Seen at Minffordd on 19 April 2007 and designed to emulate its Victorian predecessors, it entered service in 1992, and has burnt coal from 2014. *Author*

LEFT Completion of the Welsh Highland Railway sees the regular appearance of Garratts at Porthmadog. No 138 spent the night at Boston Lodge on 19 April 2011. *Author*

LEFT Since the FR was restored to Blaenau Ffestiniog in 1982 a great deal of effort has been spent on restoring original lineside features. Penrhyn station, seen with *Merddin Emrys* passing on 5 May 2007, now serves as a volunteers' hostel. *Author*

ABOVE A pair of Fairlies at Boston Lodge on 5 May 2007, with *David Lloyd George* being prepared for service on the pit while single Fairlie *Taliesin* shunts in the background. More than 200 subscribers paid for the construction of *Taliesin* at Boston Lodge between 1989 and 1999. The original single Fairlie of this name had been built in 1876 and dismantled in 1932. *Author*

BELOW *Earl of Merioneth*, burning coal instead of oil since May 2006, passes Boston Lodge en route for Blaenau Ffestiniog on 5 May 2007. *Taliesin* waits for the token to be released before it can run to Porthmadog to take the next train. *Author*

RIGHT On 8 August 2010 the new Lynton & Barnstaple Railway Manning, Wardle 2-6-2T *Lyd* passes Boston Lodge with one of its first loaded test runs. *Author*

LEFT Heading for the hills, *Blanche* crosses Madocks's embankment on 29 March 2009. In the background, the old locomotive sheds had recently been restored. *Author*

BELOW The three-year project to enlarge the FR's Porthmadog station to accommodate the Welsh Highland Railway was completed in 2014. On 19 April *Merddin Emrys* returns from Blaenau Ffestiniog while a WHR train stands at the enlarged and realigned platform. *Author*

Two railways with Acts of Parliament were built to the 2ft 3in gauge. The **Corris Railway** and Talyllyn Railway were located quite close together on the borders of Merionethshire and Montgomeryshire, where they served quarries that worked the same slate veins.

The first was opened as the Corris, Machynlleth & River Dovey Tramroad in 1859, pursuant to a series of Acts of Parliament enacted between 1852 and 1858. Its traffic originated from slate quarries at Aberllefenni and Ratgoed, and it ran for 7½ miles down the Dulas valley to reach wharves on the banks of the Dyfi, at Morben and Derwenlas near the market town of Machynlleth. There was a branch line to more quarries at Upper Corris.

In common with the Festiniog Railway, loaded trains were worked by gravity, with horses returning the empty wagons to the quarries. Sometime in 1863/64 the railway was acquired by the contractor, Thomas Savin, who tried to sell it to the Aberystwyth & Welsh Coast Railway. When this line was opened in 1863 the narrow gauge line to the wharves fell out of use. The railway's name was changed to the Corris Railway by an 1864 Act, when power to use steam locomotives was obtained.

Savin's bankruptcy in 1866 put the railway into limbo until it was sold to the Tramways & General Works Company, then to Imperial Tramways in 1878. An agreement was made for the first to reconstruct and equip the railway for locomotive working and passenger carrying on behalf of the second.

Although the carrying of passengers was expressly forbidden by the railway's 1864 Act, they had probably been carried unofficially since the railway opened; from 1874 until 1879, when the practice stopped, the numbers carried were included in official returns. One of the quarry-owners objected to the carriage of passengers for fear that it would interfere with the slate traffic, but another Act gave permission in 1880. When the inspecting officer attended in October, however, he refused to approve the railway's use by passengers because it was partly built beyond the limits of deviation, the curves were too sharp and the clearances too tight.

It took three years, and another Act, before the railway obtained the Board of Trade's approval to carry passengers the 5 miles between Machynlleth and Corris. Tramways & General Works had supplied the railway with three Hughes 0-4-0STs and eight four-wheeled tramway-style carriages. The limited clearances were dealt with by only allowing access to the trains from one side. From 1888 the railway started a programme of improving its carriage stock by buying bogie carriages and by mounting pairs of original carriages onto bogie underframes. The locomotives were improved by the addition of trailing pony trucks.

ABOVE The Corris Railway's bridge across the Dyfi proved to be its undoing when the railway was owned by British Railways. When flooding in 1948 threatened to wash out the ground behind the abutments the line was closed immediately. The bridge had been rebuilt in the form shown in 1906. The presence of a figure standing by the back of the train suggests that it had been stopped for the photographer. *WHS Series*

During its horse/gravity days the railway had been very profitable. The increased costs associated with steam traction reduced its profitability considerably and it was subsidised by Imperial Tramways. Tourism was an essential part of the railway's business and it ran horse buses from Corris to Talyllyn in connection with the trains. Passenger services were extended from Corris to Aberllefenni, 1½ miles, in 1887.

Some significant investments were made in the 20th century. Machynlleth station was replaced in 1904/05, the Dovey river bridge was renewed in 1906, and a Kerr, Stuart 'Tattoo' 0-4-2ST was purchased in 1921. Charabancs had been used on the road service since 1910 and the routes expanded to cover Aberystwyth, Dolgellau and Abergynolwyn as well as Talyllyn.

The Great Western Railway's purchase of the line for £1,000 in 1929 was a condition of a transaction to purchase the Bristol Tramways & Carriage Company, a company that had links to Imperial Tramways. The most obvious change to the railway was the withdrawal of passenger services from 1 January 1931. Two of the carriages were sold to owners in Gobowen, and the remainder were scrapped.

The railway survived until August 1948, just after it had been nationalised. Heavy rain threatened to undermine the Dyfi river bridge and the traffic did not justify the cost of repair. The track was dismantled by 1951 and the two remaining locomotives were kept in store at Machynlleth, allegedly in contradiction of an instruction to send them to Swindon for scrapping, until they were sold to the Talyllyn Railway for £25 each in 1951.

Moves to preserve and restore the railway followed the establishment of a society in 1966. A museum was opened in the old railway stable block at Corris in 1970 and a train service was started between Corris and the original locomotive shed at Maespoeth, just under a mile, in 2002. In 2005 a new Kerr, Stuart 'Tattoo' 0-4-2ST was commissioned. Built by members, a carriage shed at Maespoeth was completed in 2009 and construction of three new carriages has been started there.

Plans to extend southwards to Tan y coed, near Esgairgeiliog, and to build a new station at Corris are being developed. The steam locomotive fleet will be increased with the addition of a Hughes 0-4-2ST that is under construction.

ABOVE One of the Corris Railway's Hughes 0-4-2STs stands with a short goods train at Machynlleth. The removal of the vacuum brake dates the photograph to the later 1930s, after the passenger services had ceased in 1931. *A. E. Rimmer*

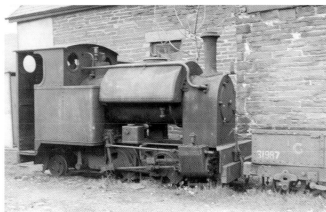

LEFT In 1921 Corris Railway No 4, a Kerr, Stuart 'Tattoo' 0-4-2ST, was the last new locomotive supplied to the railway. Photographed at Machynlleth on 30 April 1950, a year later it was sold to the Talyllyn Railway with its shedmate, Hughes 0-4-2ST No 3.

RIGHT The official reopening of the Corris Railway between Corris and Maespoeth on 7 June 2003 was marked by the loan of a Corris train by the Talyllyn Railway for a month. The train comprised a carriage, coal wagon, brake van and Hughes 0-4-2ST No 3, the latter seen at Maespoeth on the reopening day. The TR had loaned the Kerr, Stuart 'Tattoo' 0-4-2ST No 4 for 10 days in 1996. *Author*

LEFT Beyond the limits of the present Corris Railway operation there are still signs of the old railway to be found – Machynlleth station building and the slate-fenced formation between Corris and Aberllefenni, for example. This stone bridge, in the centre of the Corris, carried the railway on to Aberllefenni. *Author*

About 4 miles from Corris, the Bryn Eglwys quarries tapped the same slate veins as the Corris area quarries. The natural outlet for their slate, though, was the harbour at Aberdovey. From 1866 it was routed to a wharf on the Cambrian Railways' line on the Cardigan Bay coast at Tywyn via the **Talyllyn Railway**, which was also 2ft 3in gauge. The quarry company owned the railway company.

The route was surveyed in 1864 by James Swinton Spooner, a son of the Festiniog Railway's Charles Easton Spooner, and construction was started soon afterwards. The Act of Parliament was obtained in 1865. The contractor has not been identified but might well have been Thomas Savin or one of his sub-contractors.

With an inland terminus at Abergynolwyn, 242 feet above sea level, the line was 6½ miles long. The quarries were connected by a mineral siding and inclines. An incline down from the siding enabled heavier goods to be delivered to the village, which was about half a mile from the station. The steepest gradient is a short stretch of 1 in 69 at Ty Mawr. At Dolgoch, a 51-foot-high, three-arch viaduct crosses a ravine.

The Cumbrian firm of Fletcher, Jennings supplied the railway with two locomotives of very difference appearance, an 0-4-0ST in 1864 and an 0-4-0WT in 1866. Named *Talyllyn* and *Dolgoch* respectively, the first was soon modified to 0-4-2ST to improve its stability. Four four-wheeled carriages and a van provided the passenger accommodation. An unusual feature of the van was the inclusion of a booking office window for the sale of tickets at intermediate stations. Another carriage was obtained in 1870.

Goods services started as soon as construction allowed, with passenger services following in December 1866. The government inspector had refused to approve the latter because clearances through the overbridges were too tight, but this was resolved by moving the track over to one side and screwing the carriage doors closed on that side.

The quarries and their railway were not the busiest in Wales and no other rolling stock was required. In 1911 the local MP, Henry Haydn Jones, purchased the railway and quarries as a personal job creation/maintenance scheme, and kept them going until his death in 1950. In 1935 he had taken a seven-year lease on the Aberllefenni slate quarry to keep the Corris Railway open.

ABOVE A Talyllyn Railway train is seen at Pendre circa 1903. The differences between the locomotives, ordered a year apart from the same builder, are very evident here. The first was *Talyllyn*, delivered as an 0-4-0ST but soon altered to 0-4-2ST, while the second was 0-4-0WT *Dolgoch*. The photographer must have arranged for them to be posed thus, for the railway never had enough traffic to require the use of both together. The wrinkling of *Dolgoch*'s cab is because it has been made with plate that is too light for its purpose. The carriage doors are sealed on this side because of the restricted clearance through the railway's overbridges. *H. Fayle*

After Jones's death Tom Rolt and his friends persuaded his executors to hand over the railway to the newly formed Talyllyn Railway Preservation Society. Rolt was an enthusiast for traditional technologies and deplored their loss in the face of post-war modernisation.

On 14 May 1951 the railway was run with the support of volunteers, the first in the world to do so. Public response was good, encouraging them to make the effort required to overcome the ravages of time on the original rolling stock and rail that was still in use. All was extremely worn out and needed to be repaired and replaced in the interest of safety.

Over the next 40 years new locomotives and carriages were acquired, built and restored. The most notable acquisitions were two locomotives, one bogie carriage and several wagons formerly used on the Corris Railway, and two Glyn Valley Tramway carriages. A 3-foot-gauge Barclay was bought from Ireland and parts of it were used in a new locomotive built in the railway's own works at Pendre. Eight bogie carriages were among those built by the railway in the 1960s and '70s.

Facilities throughout the railway were improved, and in 1976, after six years' work, the line was extended three-quarters of a mile over the mineral line to a new station at Nant Gwernol, the extension authorised by means of a Light Railway Order. With support from the Heritage Lottery Fund, a substantial new station at Towyn was opened by HRH the Prince of Wales and the Duchess of Cornwall in 2005 and accommodates the Narrow Gauge Railway Museum as well as the booking hall, shop and café. Under-cover storage at Pendre was supplemented by a new stock shed at Quarry Siding in 2012.

RIGHT The wharf at Towyn (now Tywyn) was not intended for passenger trains and the track closest to the office building runs over the weighbridge. Until around 1918 passenger trains started at Pendre. As late as the 1930s loaded wagons were run into the station by gravity. The building on the extreme right is the explosives store.

LEFT Named *Pretoria* during the Boer War, the second locomotive passes Pendre with a mixed train in about 1911. A gunpowder wagon stands on the right. *G. M. Perkins*

LEFT Trains still stop at Dolgoch to take water, although the archaic water tower with its wooden trough is rarely used. This scene dates from the 1920s. *Frith*

7205

ABOVE The rustic charm of Abergynolwyn, the original passenger terminus, has now been lost. Seen here circa 1930, the photographer's bike is propped against the waiting shelter.

RIGHT The passenger terminus was distant from the village that it served, but the railway did serve the village in a rather unusual manner, via an incline and a siding that were used to deliver goods and collect the euphemistic 'night soil'. The incline was connected to the railway's mineral branch, the three-quarter-mile extension along the Nant Gwernol towards the Bryn Eglwys quarries. *Park*

Abergynolwyn Village.

RIGHT The end of the mineral line. By 1950 the entire railway was grass-covered like this.

RIGHT Overhauled at the Atlas Foundry, Shrewsbury, in 1945, *Dolgoch* was the only locomotive that worked when photographed at Abergynolwyn on 25 August 1948. Its cab still looks a bit battered. *H. C. Casserley*

LEFT In 1951 the Talyllyn Railway became the first to be run by a society with volunteers in operating roles, but a great deal of effort was required to make the railway viable. The last two Corris Railway locomotives were purchased from British Railways in 1951. Corris No 3, an 0-4-2ST built by Hughes in Loughborough in 1878, was put into service facing downhill, as its cab could only be accessed from one side. Photographed in July 1953, alterations from its Corris condition were cosmetic, and it had been named *Sir Haydn* after the TR's former owner.

LEFT The second Corris Railway locomotive was a Kerr, Stuart 'Tattoo' 0-4-2ST. It entered service on the TR in 1952 after an overhaul carried out free of charge by the Hunslet company in Leeds, that company owning the Kerr, Stuart goodwill. It was named *Edward Thomas* after the last manager of the old regime. Despite the grass the sleepers look as though they have been replaced.

LEFT The railway's use of internal combustion motive power was cautious, involving the adaptation of machines not designed for the purpose. No 7 had been a Mercury tractor and was introduced in 1954, but only lasted until 1957.
J. J. Davies

RIGHT On a crisp January day in 1966 *Edward Thomas* makes a brisk run up the line with bogie carriage No 9 and the Corris Railway brake van. From 1958 until 1969 this locomotive was at the forefront of steam locomotive technology as it was fitted with a Giesl ejector and its associated slimline chimney.

RIGHT The three-quarter-mile mineral extension beyond Abergynolwyn exerted a strong pull on the early TR members and volunteers. Work started on the formation to make it suitable for passenger trains in 1970, and it opened on 22 May 1976. On the opening day the author organised a train that became the first to run through Abergynolwyn non-stop and the first charter train to the new terminus. The untouched formation was photographed in 1963.

ABOVE Nant Gwernol is the starting point for a series of footpaths, the tranquil location being appreciated by many passengers. *Edward Thomas* is running round on 22 August 1992.

BELOW With exponential traffic growth in the 1960s the railway needed to ensure that it had adequate motive power, so in 1969 it bought a 3-foot-gauge Barclay 0-4-0WT from the Irish Turf Board, Bord Na Móna, which could supply components for a new locomotive. Work started at Pendre in 1972, but as the passengers discovered the delights of cheap overseas holidays it ceased to be a priority and work progressed at intervals until

the locomotive entered service on 6 May 1991. Originally named *Irish Pete*, a pun on its origins, on a second vote in 1989 the name of the man who instigated the railway's preservation, Tom Rolt, gained precedence over Cader Idris.

In the 1890s the TR had resisted the Board of Trade's requirements over compliance with the 1889 Regulation of Railways Act and the use of continuous brakes, pleading poverty and threatening to close the railway if the board insisted. Eventually, the railway responded to the subtle pressure applied by the board's successors and brought air brakes into use from 1993. The locomotive was photographed on 26 July 2013. *Author*

LEFT The original locomotives catch the sun at Tywyn on 14 May 2011, as the railway celebrated the 60th anniversary of its preservation. *Dolgoch* was being launched back into traffic, having been rebuilt with a new boiler that had been paid for by external organisations, including the Science Museum's PRISM fund and the readers of *Steam Railway* magazine. *Author*

RIGHT This tableau, photographed on 28 May 2013, has been created in the corner behind the old gunpowder store at Towyn, incorporating the original weighbridge into a weigh house of typical Welsh style. *Author*

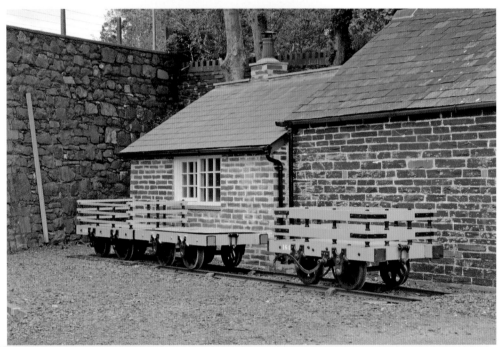

RIGHT Working with a contractor, the Talyllyn Railway completed an extensive overhaul of Barclay 0-4-0WT *Douglas* in 2013. Turned out in this bright red livery, it is seen leaving Abergynolwyn on 26 July. *Douglas*'s appearance as the Awdry character locomotive *Duncan* is very popular with the railway's young visitors. *Author*

ABOVE After many years of prevarication and indecision over what was desirable or achievable, the buildings at Tywyn were subject to considerable change in a project that was partially funded by the Heritage Lottery Fund. Seen on 22 July 2001, the museum building had become rather tired, and the catering department and manager's office were accommodated in portable buildings. *Author*

BELOW These issues were addressed in a project that was commemorated by a visit by HRH the Prince of Wales and the Duchess of Cornwall on 13 July 2005. This photograph was taken on 4 May 2007. *Author*

Although it was built without Parliamentary powers, there was a third 2ft 3in-gauge railway not too far away, in Cardiganshire, that is worth mentioning. The **Plynlimon & Hafan Tramway** ran from the Cambrian Railways' yard at Llanfihangel, 6 miles from Aberystwyth, to the Hafan lead mine, 7 miles away, continuing thence, via an incline, to a granite quarry 1½ miles further on, both on the flanks on Plynlimon.

Although construction was started in 1893, a goods service was not started until 1897. On 15 April the *Aberystwyth Observer* forecast a formal opening taking place in June. Despite a successful trial with the passenger carriage in August, it was not until 28 March 1898 that a Mondays-only (market day) passenger service was started. By 19 August, however, the *Cambrian News* was reporting that all services had been suspended 'for want of adequate patronage'. All services were suspended in December 1898. A year later the *Cambrian News* was still extolling the value of the line for tourists, especially if a road was made from Hafan to the summit of Plynlimon, 2,468 feet. Winding-up proceedings were started in December 1899.

The railway had had only two locomotives, one bogie carriage and a few wagons. One of the locomotives and the wagons were sold to the contractor building the Vale of Rheidol Railway.

Built to a 2ft 4½in gauge and 6 miles long, the **Glyn Valley Tramway** ran between Chirk and Glyn Ceiriog in Denbighshire. Its Act was obtained in 1870, although there had been two precursors. It was opened in 1873 for the carriage of goods and minerals, including slate and granite, and in 1874 for passengers. From Pontfaen, a mile from Chirk, the line climbed from 287 to 552 feet above sea level. The steepest gradient on this part of the line was a short section of 1 in 45 just before the terminus. Between Chirk and Pontfaen there was a section with a falling gradient ranging from 1 in 40 to 1 in 50. At Chirk traffic was exchanged with the Great Western Railway or the Shropshire Union Canal. Haulage was initially by horses, with passengers riding in wagons before three four-wheeled carriages were put into service.

The route was a roadside tramway, which placed limitations on the use of steam locomotives. From 1887 the line was rebuilt to make it suitable, and in 1888 goods haulage started using two 0-4-2T tram engines obtained from Beyer, Peacock; they had their motion concealed to reduce the risk of frightening livestock on the road. After a five-year interval, passenger services were resumed in 1891, 14 more four-wheeled carriages being purchased over the next ten years. A third tram engine was obtained in 1892, and in 1921 an ex-War Department Baldwin 4-6-0PT was re-gauged from 2 feet and put into service.

The inter-war depression and increased use of motor vehicles finished the passenger traffic in 1933, and the goods traffic ended two years later. The locomotives were scrapped and the carriages sold for non-rail use locally. In the 1950s two were rescued and restored by the Talyllyn Railway.

Two organisations with different objectives have taken an interest in the tramway and its remains. In 2012 one of them obtained planning permission to construct a railway on the section between Chirk and Pontfaen.

BELOW As always, the presence of a train and a camera attract children. The Glyn Valley Tramway's Beyer, Peacock locomotive was named after Sir Theodore Martin, the company chairman when it was delivered in 1888. He was also a local landowner and friend of Queen Victoria. There are wagons attached to the train beyond the carriages. *Gwenfro Series*

ABOVE A train hauled by one of the Glyn Valley Tramway's Beyer, Peacock tram engines waits at the Glyn Ceiriog terminus. The locomotive shed, in the centre of the picture, survives, albeit with different doors and having lost its ventilation cowls when it was reroofed with asbestos panels. The dog-leg in the track leading to the shed indicates the location of the turntable. There are wagons stabled on the line to the right, which served the Wynne and Cambrian quarries. More quarries were accessed beyond the station. 'Efrydfa', the house on the right, was completed in 1892. *Unique Series*

ABOVE One of the tram engines shunts granite wagons at Chirk. The Great Western Railway station is beyond the fence on the left.

ABOVE Slate being transhipped at Chirk in 1925. *H. G. W. Household*

LEFT A mixed train stands at Pontfadog in 1932. The locomotive was named after Henry Dennis, a Cornish surveyor and mining engineer who was one of the tramway's instigators and its engineer. *H. C. Casserley*

35

Thirty miles from the GVT, a mineral railway in Shropshire also used the same gauge. Authorised in 1873, the **Snailbeach District Railways** was built to serve lead mines in the Stiperstones, near Pontesbury, south-west of Shrewsbury; from 1905 its main traffic was granite. Opened in 1887, it was 3½ miles long and never carried passengers. It exchanged traffic at Pontesbury on the Great Western Railway's Minsterley branch.

After steam haulage ended in 1946, traction was provided by an agricultural tractor, a practice that continued when Shropshire County Council leased the line in 1947. The quarry being made accessible to lorries in 1959, the trackbed was used as a private road and the track was scrapped. The railway company continued in existence and the county council continued to pay for using the railway until a new access road was built in 1998. There appeared to have been no interest when the company had been advertised for sale in 1984, and a restoration scheme that surfaced on the internet in 2007/08 appeared to be without foundation.

ABOVE Photographed in about 1925, this view of the Snailbeach District Railways' primitive engine shed is as close to the railway's heyday as can be found. On the right is the Bagnall 0-6-0T *Dennis*, delivered in 1906. The only working locomotive when Colonel Stephens took over the line in 1922, it was soon dismantled for an overhaul that was never completed.

LEFT Superficially the same scene as that illustrated on above, close examination shows that the photograph was taken on a different occasion. The locomotives are not as well cared for and the engine shed has lost a part of its roof.

RIGHT This is the interchange with the Great Western Railway's Minsterley branch at Pontesbury. The high-level siding was for outgoing minerals, the low-level for incoming coal and other back traffic.

LEFT This Kerr, Stuart 0-4-2T, which arrived at Snailbeach in 1922, had been 2ft 6in gauge when built in 1902. It had been used by the Admiralty at Ridham, Kent, during the war, then at the Central Stores Depot in Neasden.

LEFT The SDR had two ex-War Department Baldwin 4-6-0Ts that had been rebuilt by Bagnall in 1918, arriving at Snailbeach in 1923. No 722 was photographed shortly after delivery; it later lost its chimney cover and cast number plates. The large pipe to the water tank is the feed from the water lifter, which enabled water to be taken from a stream. When the locomotives became disused in 1946 they were abandoned outside the locomotive shed until they were cut up on site in 1950.

ESKDALE EXPRESS, BOOT.

ABOVE One of the Ravenglass & Eskdale Railway's Manning, Wardle 0-6-0Ts stands at Boot with a train consisting of the railway's entire original passenger stock, two coaches and a brake van supplied by the Bristol Wagon Company. Stabled in the ore-loading siding is the 'big saloon', built locally for peak-time use. Judging by the positioning of the windows, high in the body sides, users were not expected to enjoy the experience.

Only two public 3-foot-gauge railways were built in England, the Ravenglass & Eskdale Railway, on the west coast in Cumbria, and the Southwold Railway on the east coast in Suffolk. Another coastal 3-foot-gauge line, the Rye & Camber Tramway, was built without statutory authority and opened in 1895. In Scotland the Aluminium Corporation had an extensive 3-foot-gauge system serving its works near Fort William. Much greater use was made of this gauge in the Isle of Man and Ireland.

The **Ravenglass & Eskdale Railway** was opened from an interchange with the Furness Railway at Ravenglass and ran 7 miles eastwards, terminating at Boot. It was promoted by the Whitehaven Iron Mines Company, which owned one of several iron ore mines in the area. Authorised by an Act of Parliament in 1873, it was opened in 1875, equipped with just one Manning, Wardle 0-6-0T.

A second locomotive was obtained from Manning, Wardle in 1876, when the Bristol Wagon Company supplied two passenger carriages and a brake van. A third carriage was built locally. All were four-wheeled. The passenger service was started on 20 November 1876.

Being unable to pay the contractor and evidently unable to place the £12,000 additional capital authorised by the Board of Trade in March 1876, the railway was placed in receivership in 1877. Mineral traffic peaked at 9,138 tons in that year and, following the collapse of one of the mining companies, fell to less than 1,000 tons in ten years. Passenger traffic, on the other hand, grew to 21,733 by 1880 and generally ranged between 20,000 and 30,000 thereafter; however, it was insufficient to offset the loss of the mineral traffic.

Remaining in receivership, the railway struggled; its stock was ill-maintained and decrepit. A proposal for the Furness Railway to take over its operation in 1898 came to nothing. At the end of the 1908 season the railway was in such a poor condition that it was closed.

In 1909 powers were obtained to create a new company to take over the assets of the old and to raise funds to reconstruct the railway for passenger traffic. Before they came into effect one of the quarries

took a six-month lease on the line. When it expired at the end of the year the Eskdale Railway Company took over. Despite the optimism, no fresh capital was forthcoming and the railway was not rebuilt.

Trains were run by the company in 1910, then in 1911 it was leased again and thereafter was worked spasmodically, dependent on the stone available. From 30 April 1913 it was abandoned.

In 1915 it was taken over by Narrow Gauge Railways Ltd, a vehicle for the rail products of the Northamptonshire modelmaker W. Bassett-Lowke. In 1916 the same group took on the 2-foot-gauge horse tramway at Fairbourne, near Barmouth in Wales, and also converted it to the 15-inch gauge.

In Cumbria, it subsequently appeared that the Eskdale Railway director who made the transaction with NGR had no authority to do so and did not disburse the receipts to creditors and shareholders as he should have done. Notwithstanding, the line was converted to the 15-inch gauge using the original rails and sleepers.

Bassett-Lowke supplied locomotives and rolling stock. Additional equipment was obtained from the late Sir Arthur Heywood's 15-inch-gauge demonstration line at Duffield Bank, Derbyshire. In Eskdale the scale engineering was found to be unsuitable for everyday work, and new, more heavily-built and powerful locomotives were built for the line.

Although a year-round service was operated, the main source of traffic was tourists. The Beckfoot quarry was reopened in 1922, providing additional traffic. Local landowner and Cunard shipping magnate Sir Aubrey Brocklebank, a Narrow Gauge Railways Ltd

RIGHT Delivered in 1875, *Devon* was the first locomotive on the line. Around 20 years later it was rebuilt by the Lowca Engineering Company at nearby Whitehaven; that company's rebuild plate is attached to the edge of the running board. Seen at Eskdale Green station, the presence of the bicycle dates the photograph to the early years of the 20th century.

debenture holder, took over the company in 1925 and it was amalgamated with the quarry company in 1928/29. The combined concern was to be taken over by the Keswick Granite Company of Threlkeld in 1949.

From 1929 an unusual feature of the line was the operation of standard gauge wagons to the stone crusher at Murthwaite, 2½ miles from Ravenglass, to eliminate double-handling. Rails for the standard gauge were laid outside the 15-inch gauge, and a Kerr, Stuart diesel locomotive was acquired to work the traffic.

With the closure of the quarry, the railway was offered for sale in 1957 but not sold until 1960, when an auction was held. Under new management a new company was formed and the preservation ethos adopted, with volunteers participating in the railway's operation.

Now owned by a family trust, the Ravenglass & Eskdale Railway has undergone many changes and improvements since 1960. Two new steam locomotives and several diesels have been put into service and the passenger experience enhanced with the introduction of enclosed carriages. The terminal facilities have been replaced and modernised and the railway owns the adjoining standard gauge railway station building, which it converted into a popular pub. There is no way that the original promoters could have imagined how their railway would have developed to survive into the 21st century.

BELOW The other Manning, Wardle 0-6-0T was delivered in 1876. Named *Nabb Gill*, it was photographed at Ravenglass.

„Nabb Gill", The Eskdale Express.   Ravenglass

ABOVE *Devon* heads briskly up the valley with a goods train after 1898, when its air pump was fitted.

RIGHT The scale of this derailment gives an indication of the poor condition of the railway near Murthwaite when it happened on 10 March 1905. The photograph also indicates that some exchange of components between the locomotives had taken place, for barely discernible on the tank is the name *Devon*, but the position of the air pump reveals that the locomotive is *Nabb Gill*; the air pumps were of different sides.

Eskdale Express derailed at Murthwaite

RIGHT The railway closed in 1913 and was taken over by Narrow Gauge Railways Ltd in 1915. The first 15-inch-gauge locomotive to be used was 4-4-2 *Sans Pareil*, seen heading up the valley on the re-gauged original track.

RIGHT Bassett-Lowke 4-6-2 *Colossus* had been built as *John Anthony* for Captain John Howey for his railway at Staughton Manor, Cambridgeshire, in 1914. It cost £400 when purchased for the Ravenglass & Eskdale Railway in 1916. It was badly damaged in a head-on collision in 1925 and withdrawn in 1927, although its frames and wheelsets were to be reused in another locomotive. With the Furness Railway's River Mite viaduct in the background, the train is approaching the Barrow Marsh on the climb out of Ravenglass. *W. J. Bassett-Lowke*

LEFT In 1916/17 three locomotives and other equipment that had been built by Sir Arthur Heywood for trials on his Duffield Bank estate in Derbyshire were obtained. 0-6-0T *Ella* had been built in 1881 and its frames and wheels were reused when Internal Combustion Locomotive No 2 was built in 1927. It was obviously a busy day when this photograph was taken, for the passengers are riding in stone trucks. The 3-foot-gauge waiting shelter was still in use. *Ravenglass & Eskdale Railway*

LEFT 15-inch-gauge services were briefly operated to Boot, but the 1 in 36 gradient was too steep for the locomotives. Services were cut back to Beckfoot before being extended into the disused Gill Force mineral branch to terminate outside Dalegarth cottages. Until a turntable was installed in 1923/24 trains returned to Ravenglass with their engines running tender-first. Although two of the cottages were converted to provide passenger facilities, in 1926 the terminus was moved to a more convenient location along the branch by the main road and requirements were provided there. *G. P. Abraham*

E 830-201 ESKDALE MINIATURE RAILWAY.

LEFT Standard gauge track was laid as far as the Murthwaite crushing plant in 1929. Although it remained in situ for more than 30 years it was rarely photographed, and no photographs of standard gauge trains have come to light. 0-8-2 *River Irt* was built in 1927, using the chassis from the Heywood 0-8-0T *Ursula*, which had been acquired in 1917. *Sankey's Photo Press*

RIGHT Henry Greenly designed 2-8-2 *River Esk* to haul stone trains on the RER. The first 2-8-2 to operate in Britain, it was built by Davey, Paxman in 1923. This early 1950s scene is notable because the company-owned Kerr, Stuart standard gauge diesel locomotive is visible, to the left of the flag pole. Purchased in 1929, it was sold in 1955 and is preserved on the Foxfield Railway in Staffordshire. *G. P. Abraham*

2. Ravenglass Station. Ravenglass & Eskdale Rly.

RIGHT A train passes the Murthwaite plant while it was still operational. The site has become extensively overgrown since it fell out of use.

ABOVE In this busy scene at Muncaster Mill on 6 May 1996, the train engine is 2-8-2 *River Mite*, built for the Ravenglass & Eskdale Railway Preservation Society in 1966 by Clarkson in York using parts from an earlier locomotive. *Author*

BELOW *River Esk* arrives at Irton Road in August 1975.

LEFT A Southwold Railway mixed train is in the course of loading at Southwold. The locomotive is one of the railway's Sharp, Stewart 2-4-0s, No 3 *Blyth*. The timber platforms favoured by the Southwold Railway were not found on other narrow gauge lines. The carriage shed was erected in 1902. *Frith*

The **Southwold Railway** served a resort on the Suffolk coast, 8¾ miles from the market town of Halesworth, where the terminus was adjacent to the Great Eastern Railway station. Unusually, its construction was not motivated by the carriage of minerals; in addition to carrying passengers and goods, the railway's ability to carry fish enabled Southwold to compete with Lowestoft and other East Coast ports.

Authorised by an Act of Parliament in 1876, it was opened on 24 September 1879; construction had been delayed by the difficulty in raising capital and acquiring the land, and had only been started in June of that year. The contractor was Charles Chambers, who in 1890 was to rebuild the Potteries, Shrewsbury & North Wales Railway for the Shropshire Railways. On the first day services were immediately suspended because of flooding at Wenhaston.

Sharp, Stewart supplied three 2-4-0Ts, and six tramcar-style carriages with Cleminson six-wheeled flexible underframes were obtained from the Bristol Wagon Works. Just short of Southwold the railway crossed the River Blythe on a swing bridge, an Admiralty requirement despite the absence of vessels using the river.

An application to the Board of Trade for powers to raise additional capital was made in November 1879 but the certificate was not issued until 1888, after three more applications. The railway paid its way and passenger numbers slowly increased.

The situation was sufficiently stable to consider expansion, and in 1902 a Light Railway Order was made authorising an extension to Kessingland, Lowestoft, 9 miles away. It would have been standard gauge to facilitate the exchange of traffic with the Great Eastern Railway; authority was given to convert the existing railway and to work it as a light railway as well. Several bridges, including the swing bridge, were altered to accommodate the wider gauge but the extension was not built.

A shorter 1-mile extension was built to the harbour, an initiative of the Southwold Harbour Company, which obtained the necessary Light Railway Order in 1913. It was more steeply graded than the main line, and in 1914 a Manning, Wardle 0-6-2T was obtained to work it.

The First World War had a limited effect on the railway. There was troop traffic, some wagons were damaged by an incendiary bomb, and it was used to transport 680 Dutch stranded in England by the war – the Germans guaranteed safe conduct only if Southwold harbour was used. There were enough profits to pay a small dividend and to have the carriages overhauled.

In the late 1920s bus competition was increased, the weather was poor, and passenger numbers fell rapidly. Rightly or wrongly, the railway gained a reputation for bucolic shambolism and two sets of postcards produced by a local artist illustrating it in this form found a ready market. A writer in *The Times* said that the railway should not be mocked for it was the making of Southwold. However, after appeals for financial assistance failed, the last train ran on 11 April 1929, all but 50 years after the first.

The company was put into receivership and the railway abandoned, left in limbo. The receiver could not dispose of the assets of a statutory company and there were no funds to apply for an abandonment order. In 1941 the assets were requisitioned for the war effort and all that was moveable had gone within a few months.

Thanks to some judicial inflexibility the company was left in suspense until 1992, when it was registered as a limited company under the Companies Act and finally liquidated. A society formed to investigate the possibility of reviving the railway in 1994 became a charitable trust in 2006; it is promoting the development of a railway centre at Wenhaston and the construction of a replica locomotive.

ABOVE No 3 *Blyth* is seen with goods stock at Southwold circa 1908. The plate above the number plate indicates that the locomotive was rebuilt with a new boiler in 1900, the work being carried out at Southwold. Another new boiler was installed in 1925. The well-loaded wagon next to the locomotive is a six-wheeled Cleminson vehicle. *F. Jenkins*

RIGHT The Southwold Railway exchanged traffic with the Great Eastern Railway at Halesworth, and for a short distance the lines ran parallel. No 3 *Blyth* and railway personnel pose for the camera; the absence of continuous brakes means that the photograph predates compliance with the 1889 Regulation of Railways Act.

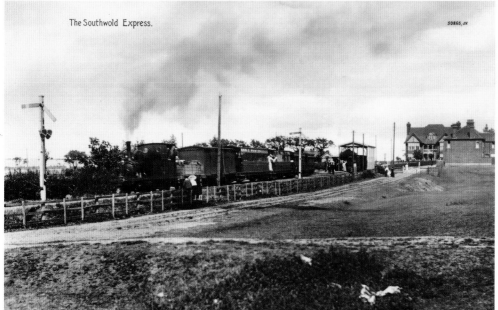

The Southwold Express.

LEFT Children stand on the fence to watch a train leave Southwold circa 1905. The signal posts accommodate both home and starting signals. *Valentine*

LEFT An extreme alternative view of the 'Southwold Express' was developed by a local artist who published 12 postcards of his impressions. *Reg Carter*

THE SOUTHWOLD EXPRESS   A COW ON THE LINE IS LUCKILY SEEN BY THE GUARD - IN HIS EAGERNESS TO STOP THE TRAIN HE PUTS THE BRAKES ON TOO SUDDENLY !

Moving to Devon, the **Lynton & Barnstaple Railway** was opened in 1898, the ultimate 19th-century British 2-foot-gauge railway. Linking the market town of Barnstaple with the twin resorts of Lynton and Lynmouth, it literally roamed 20 miles across wildest Exmoor to do so.

Authorised by an 1895 Act of Parliament, its promoters included the publisher Sir George Newnes, who owned a house at Lynton set in 40 acres. At Barnstaple there was a cross-platform interchange with the London & South Western Railway's Ilfracombe branch. Gradients as steep as 1 in 50 were required to reach the 1,000-foot summit at Woody Bay, before falling to 700 feet at Lynton. The most noteworthy feature was an eight-arch brick viaduct at Chelfham, 70 feet high. The station buildings were notable for their Swiss chalet style.

Manning, Wardle supplied three 2-6-2Ts named *Exe*, *Taw* and *Yeo* after local rivers. In 1898 the American Baldwin company supplied a 2-4-2T named *Lyn*; delivered in kit form, it was assembled by railway personnel in Barnstaple.

Sixteen handsome bogie carriages were obtained from Bristol Carriage & Wagon, arguably the best to be found on any narrow gauge railway at that time; 39ft 6in long, eight of them had observation saloons or compartments, without windows. Only mixed trains were operated.

Constrained by gradients and curvature, the maximum load the locomotives could handle was four carriages; heavier loads required double-heading, so the railway was expensive to operate at peak times. Factors like this, and the distance of stations from the communities they served, have led to questions being asked about the promoters' intentions. Were they deliberately making sure that the railway was not too successful, to control visitor numbers to the area of Devon where they lived or had second homes? A standard gauge railway in the same terrain would have required much more substantial earthworks.

At the railway Grouping in 1923, the LBR was taken over by the Southern Railway. A programme of improvements to infrastructure and rolling stock was put in place and a new Manning, Wardle 2-6-2T, was supplied in 1925. Six carriages were fitted with steam heating in 1933. It was not enough, however – the 1920s depression and increased availability of motor transport affected traffic, and the railway was closed in 1935. Large crowds turned out to watch or ride on the last trains. The railway was soon dismantled and equipment surplus to the Southern's requirements was sold at auction. The land was sold piecemeal in 1938.

In 1979 the Lynton & Barnstaple Railway Association, a charitable trust since 2000, was formed with the objective of restoring the railway, although in places the route is blocked by developments that include a reservoir. Woody Bay station was purchased in 1995 and the short passenger railway that opened there in 2004 was extended to Killington Lane in 2006, a distance of about a mile. Plans to extend the line to serve a transport hub at Blackmoor Gate, 4 miles from Woody Bay, are being developed. Other sections of trackbed have been acquired.

Several original carriages and vans survived locally and some remain in existence. Carriage No 2 is displayed at the National Railway Museum, York, in unrestored condition, and No 15 was rebuilt by the Ffestiniog Railway as buffet car No 14. Van No 23 has been restored by the Association, and the restoration of carriages Nos 7, 16 and 17 was completed in 2013. Construction of a replica Manning, Wardle 2-6-2T, *Lyd*, was completed at the Ffestiniog Railway's Boston Lodge works in 2009. In company with No 15/14 it visited the LBR at Woody Bay in September 2010. Another Manning, Wardle and a Baldwin 2-4-2T are under construction.

RIGHT Construction of the Lynton & Barnstaple Railway began in 1896. The contractor, James Nuttall, used five locomotives, including two 3-foot-gauge Hunslet 0-4-0STs. The biggest structure on the line was the brick viaduct at Chelfham, seen with a double-headed workmen's train while still incomplete.

LEFT In preparation for the opening on 11 May 1898, two passenger trains and a crowd of employees assemble at Pilton yard, Barnstaple, for a photograph. Manning, Wardle 2-6-2T *Yeo*, on the left, hauled the first train. The other Manning, Wardle is *Exe*.

LEFT The three Manning, Wardle 2-6-2Ts supplied for the line in 1897 were notable for being named after local rivers with three-letter names, a policy that was continued with later acquisitions. At Barnstaple the platform was shared with the London & South Western Railway's line to Ilfracombe.

ABOVE Lynton station was not even convenient for the 3ft 9in-gauge water-balanced cliff lift which carries pedestrians down to the harbour. Here, *Exe* waits to return to Barnstaple with a train of three of the railway's handsome carriages.

LEFT A fourth locomotive was obtained from Baldwin in the US in 1898. A 2-4-2T named *Lyn*, it was shipped in kit form and assembled at Pilton. With a train that includes a van, it is seen here at Woody Bay, 16 miles from Barnstaple and, at 970 feet, just 12 feet below the higher of two summits on the line, which was a short distance away on the Lynton side of the station.

LEFT The Pictorial Stationery Company published a set of distinctive coloured postcards of the LBR in its appropriately named 'Peacock Series'. Blackmoor Gate, 11¾ miles from Barnstaple, was one of the stations with a chalet-style building that incorporated staff accommodation. This was the main intermediate station and trains connected with road services to Ilfracombe. *Peacock Series*

RIGHT In contrast, Snapper halt had the barest facilities. At 2¾ miles rom Barnstaple, it first appeared in Bradshaw as 'Snapper (for Goodleigh) platform' in 1904 – Goodleigh is about a mile away.

LEFT The eight-arch viaduct at Chelfham, 4¾ miles from Barnstaple, carried the railway 70 feet above the Stoke valley. In 2000 the viaduct was the subject of a £450,000 restoration scheme carried out under the aegis of the British Railways Board, the work being undertaken by a local company that incorporated the structure's original builder. *Author*

LEFT In about 1911 a short train is seen at Dean Steep, about 17 miles from Barnstaple, where the gradient is falling at 1 in 50 towards Lynton. *Valentine*

LEFT News that the LBR was to be closed prompted several newspapers to take an interest in it. Complete with a van in its train, *Yeo* was photographed in action on the curves near Snapper. The Southern Railway had numbered the LBR locomotives in 1923, and the vacuum pipes were rerouted at the front of the locomotives about six years later. *The Times*

RIGHT The LBR's stock was sold at auction on 13 November 1935, saloon/brake No 6992 (LBR No 2) becoming a summer house at Clannaborough Rectory, remaining there unaltered until it was donated to the National Railway Museum in 1982. At the museum the carriage is displayed just as it was, to demonstrate how carriages were sold for alternative uses. It is most unusual for such a vehicle to survive with its interior unaltered. Two carriages were left on rails at Snapper, 3rd Brake No 6993 (LBR No 15) being acquired by the Festiniog Railway in 1959. In Wales it was rebuilt as buffet car No 14, entering service as 'The Snapper Bar' in 1963. It was overhauled in 1997 and made a brief return visit to Devon in 2010. *Author*

BELOW Woody Bay station was reopened by the present-day Lynton & Barnstaple Railway in 2003, passenger services being resumed over a short length of track in 2004. The line was extended to Killington Lane in 2006, a distance of about a mile. *Author*

ABOVE A derelict Kerr, Stuart 'Joffre' 0-6-0WT was purchased in 1983 and parts of it were incorporated into a new 0-6-0T built at the Gartell Light Railway at Templecombe, Somerset, which entered service in 2006. *Author*

LEFT In September 2010 the LBR was host to a visit from new-build Manning, Wardle 2-6-2T *Lyd*, which had been completed at the Ffestiniog Railway's Boston Lodge works in 2009. It was a 21st-century version of the last LBR locomotives, *Lew*. For the visit it was accompanied by the FR's LBR carriage No 14 and an observation carriage. It is the railway's long-term policy to equip the railway with locomotives and carriages that are either restorations or recreations of items that originally ran on the line. The Bristol Channel and the Welsh coast are visible in the distance. *Author*

LEFT At the end of 2013 the Lynton & Barnstaple Railway put a train of three restored LBR carriages into service together with Bagnall 0-4-2T *Isaac*, which had been restored for the railway's use by a supporter. The ensemble was photographed leaving Woody Bay on 22 December. *Author*

DEVIL'S BRIDGE STATION, RHEIDOL RAILWAY, RHEIDOL VALLEY.

Returning to Wales, the **Vale of Rheidol Light Railway** was the product of an 1897 Act of Parliament that made use of Section V the 1868 Regulation of Railways Act. To encourage development this allowed a line to be worked as a light railway providing restrictions on axle loads, train speeds and level crossings were accepted.

The VRLR had a 12-mile route from the Cardigan Bay resort and fishing port of Aberystwyth, up the Rheidol valley to Devil's Bridge, the centre of the local road network that served a thinly spread community and the location of a 300-foot waterfall that attracted significant numbers of tourists. A number of ore mines were expected to provide traffic to be exported via a branch to the harbour. One of the engineers, James Weeks Szlumper, had been engineer of the North Wales Narrow Gauge Railways, a Welsh Highland Railway component, since 1891, and the Lynton & Barnstaple Railway since 1895.

As was so often the case, capital was hard to come by and progress was slow. A Light Railway Order was obtained for an extension to Aberayron in 1898 and a second Act in 1900 extended the time available for construction and the authorised capital. In 1902 a second Light Railway Order extended the time allowed for building the Aberayron extension and authorised the working of the railway as a light railway under the 1896 Light Railways Act. The Pethick brothers of Plymouth had started construction in 1901 and the line was opened on 22 December 1902.

Davies & Metcalfe supplied two 2-6-2Ts that proved to be capable of the work expected of them. From 1903 they were joined by a second-hand Bagnall 2-4-0T that had been built for export in 1896, sold to the nearby short-lived 2ft 3in-gauge Plynlimon & Hafan Railway in 1897, and used, after re-gauging, by the contractors during the VRLR's construction; it was used on lighter trains and to work the harbour branch. Twelve bogie carriages were supplied by the Midland Carriage & Wagon Company.

Notable features on the railway are the timber bridge crossing the Afon Rheidol, just over a mile from Aberystwyth, and the 1 in 50

ABOVE An off-peak scene at the Vale of Rheidol Light Railway's Devil's Bridge terminus during the railway's independent days. Bagnall 2-4-0T *Rheidol* waits while passengers board its train for the journey to the coast. In the background, on the right, a horse and cart stand at the weighbridge while timber is being loaded in the goods yard. The four-wheeled wagon in the yard, to the right of the lamp post on the left, had previously belonged to the defunct Plynlimon & Hafan Tramway. The wagon partially obscured by the station building was one of six bought in 1906. *Dennis*

gradient over the last 4 miles from Aberffrwd, 200 feet above sea level, to Devil's Bridge, at 680 feet. On the far side of the valley, a landmark created by spoil from a lead mine appears to be shaped like a stag's head.

Construction cost more than the available capital and the contractors took control of the railway. From 1905 they made several attempts to sell it to the Cambrian Railways or the GWR, and in 1910 a consortium of Cambrian directors took control, an arrangement regularised by legislation in 1913.

Traffic was a mixture of merchandise and passengers, with some minerals when the quarries were operating. In the summer the railway did well with tourists. Its big problem was that it tried to accommodate it all without adequate resources. For several summers from 1912 a locomotive was hired from the Ffestiniog Railway.

Ownership changed again in 1922, when the Cambrian was absorbed by the GWR. This meant a new station at Aberystwyth, three new locomotives and 16 new carriages. The locomotives were GWR versions of the original 2-6-2Ts, built at Swindon. The third engine, delivered in 1924, was an accountant's rebuild, given the number of its predecessor, which confused enthusiasts, and British Railways, for many years. The Bagnall was scrapped in 1924, when the harbour branch was no longer used. From 1931 the emphasis was on tourism, as the winter service was withdrawn.

British Railways took over on nationalisation in 1948 and, when steam was withdrawn from the national network in 1968, the VRLR became its last outpost in the state system. That year the narrow gauge station was relocated into the standard gauge station and the locomotives and carriages housed in the standard gauge engine shed. The locomotives and carriages were also painted in BR corporate blue livery.

British Rail could not make the line pay because the rail unions would not allow it to be treated as a tourist railway, with different conditions for the personnel concerned. A serious derailment at Nantyronen in 1986 showed that track maintenance left something to be desired. Despite this, there was some investment to aid maintenance, a personnel carrier was purchased in 1985, and a six-coupled diesel locomotive in 1987. Historic liveries were applied to the locomotives and the carriages were painted in chocolate and cream.

The idea of a sale had been mentioned in 1962, but the railway was not sold until March 1989, when it was purchased by the Brecon

Mountain Railway, which continued to manage it until 1996. Ownership was transferred to a charitable trust in 1990 and the operating company became a charity in 1999.

In private ownership most of the track has been replaced with new materials, the river bridge has been replaced and two locomotives and 15 carriages have been restored; many of the carriages have been painted in GWR livery. The passing loops at Capel Bangor and Aberffrwd have been reinstated and a programme of station improvements has been undertaken. From 2013 visitors to Devil's Bridge could participate in drive-an-engine sessions using a Kerr, Stuart 'Wren' 0-4-0ST running on a specially laid siding; a shed was constructed to house the locomotive during the 2013/4 closed season. Construction of a new workshop and engine shed at Aberystwyth was finished in 2014.

BELOW The Manchester firm of Davies & Metcalfe had been established in Aberystwyth, which might account for it receiving the order to supply two 2-6-2T locomotives, the only ones that it built. The second of them was named *Prince of Wales*. Notice the oilcan on the cylinder. The driver – 'engineman' in Cambrian Railways' parlance – was John Price Morris. He had joined the Cambrian as a cleaner at Machynlleth in 1886, aged 17, becoming

a fireman the following year, moving to Aberystwyth in 1891, and being promoted to engineman in 1896. He left the company in 1899 but returned in 1904 when he was allocated to the Vale of Rheidol. No explanation has been found for the Cambrian Railways' employing an engineman for the narrow gauge line at this time, and this appears to be the only case. Morris remained on the railway until he retired in 1928. *A. W. Croughton*

BELOW *Rheidol* stands at Aberystwyth, preparing to leave with a train of one carriage and a van. This was the only locomotive to work on the harbour branch but it was also used regularly with short trains on the Devil's Bridge service. The chimney was replaced in 1904.

LEFT When the Cambrian took over the locomotives lost their names. No 3 stands near the engine shed with brake van No 13, originally No 1, behind it.

RIGHT No 7, the first of the GWR 2-6-2Ts, stands at the first Aberystwyth station. Although the first and third carriages are in GWR livery, the second remains in the Cambrian scheme.

RIGHT A mixed train with two brake vans calls at Rheidol Falls halt. The plain roof indicates that the second carriage is one of the summer cars built by the GWR in 1923. *Frith*

RIGHT No 7 stands surrounded by the detritus of a working locomotive shed. British Railways named the Rheidol fleet in 1954.

BELOW Named after the last native Prince of Wales, No 7 crosses Park Avenue with the 2.45pm departure on 28 August 1963. *W. L. Underhay*

BELOW With the tower of St Padarn's church dominating the background, No 8 crosses the road at Llanbadarn Fawr in August 1964. The church was built in 1257, replacing an earlier building destroyed by fire. Llywelyn ap Iorwerth (1172-1240), whose name was given to No 8, was another Welsh prince, who ruled Gwynedd and had influence throughout Wales.

ABOVE No 9's driver oils round during the water stop at Aberffrwd on 17 August 1961. The locomotive was built by the GWR in 1924.

RIGHT No 8 arrives at Devil's Bridge, possibly in 1964. The plain green carriage livery with 'VofR' lettering was introduced in 1964, a poor implementation of the Cambrian scheme. It did not wear well and was replaced in 1968. *British Railways (London Midland Region)*

RIGHT In 1968 British Rail rerouted the Rheidol line from the 1925 station at Aberystwyth to the former Carmarthen line platform in the standard gauge station, which had been out of use since 1964. The realignment made the narrow gauge railway more accessible in the station and released land for sale. The work was started in February, the last train running into the old station on 16 April and the first using the new on 20 May. *G. E. Baddeley*

ABOVE Another benefit of the realignment was that the standard gauge locomotive shed could be used to accommodate the narrow gauge stock. Seen in April 1978, just as the conversion of the railway's locomotives to burn oil had started following the 1976 drought, is the exchange siding that facilitated the delivery of coal. The water tower was demolished in the 1990s. *Author*

BELOW An evening excursion in May 1981 provided an opportunity for a different photograph of a train crossing the Rheidol bridge. The structure was renewed in the same style in 1991/92, British Rail contributing £30,000 of the £105,000 cost. *Author*

ABOVE No 7 crosses the reconstructed river bridge on 14 August 1995.
Author

BELOW By July 1979 only one siding remained for stabling spare stock at Devil's Bridge. The locomotives and carriages had been painted in plain Rail Blue over the winter of 1967/68, the work carried out at Aberystwyth; it looked rather drab, and attracted much criticism.

RIGHT After 1968 the passing loops were removed from Capel Bangor and Aberffrwd. From 1976 the locomotive livery was enhanced with lining and brass 'double-arrow' logos on the cabsides. This was the scene at Aberffrwd in the summer of 1978.

LEFT With the line in private ownership from 1989, a programme of improvements was put in place. Nos 9 and 8 were overhauled at the Brecon Mountain Railway's works and the worn-out vacuum brakes were replaced by an air brake installation. The loop at Aberffrwd, seen here in the summer of 1991, was restored in 1990, and that at Capel Bangor in 2004. *Author*

LEFT A project to upgrade the railway's intermediate stations, installing platforms and reinstating buildings was completed in 2014. This was the scene at Aberffrwd on June 19, when a special train carried invited guests to view the works. In the foreground, No 9 had been repainted in Cambrian livery just a few weeks before; it retains its BR nameplates and has had its buffer plank restored to its original profile. The carriages are painted in GWR livery. *Author*

ABOVE With the increase in oil prices, coal firing was resumed in 2013. No 9's driver is oiling round while his locomotive is coaled from a South African bogie wagon on 19 July 2013. Alongside is a pair of South African bogie ballast hoppers. *Author*

BELOW As the first phase of the development of facilities at Aberystwyth, a workshop and locomotive running shed has been constructed with financial support from the Welsh Government, as seen here on 19 April 2014. *Author*

ABOVE In preparation for an event scheduled for September 2014, where the Ffestiniog Railway's England 0-4-0STT *Palmerston* was to be the star attraction, returning to the railway for the first time since 1922, a media photo-opportunity was arranged on 23 July 2014, when *Palmerston* was posed alongside No 9. *Author*

BELOW On Southampton Water, the Hythe Pier Railway train was photographed returning to Hythe on 13 August 2011. The railway's sole motive power is two Brush locomotives that were battery powered when built in 1917, the batteries being removed when they were converted to 3rd-rail pick-up in 1922. *Author*

Although it was not opened in its present form until 1922, the **Hythe Pier Railway** is a little-known line authorised by Act of Parliament in 1878. Located on the west of Southampton Water, the pier, opened in 1881, connects with a ferry to provide a transport link between Hythe and Southampton. A railway was authorised by the Act but none was built until 1909, when tracks were laid to prevent hand-propelled luggage trollies damaging the structure. Then in 1922 the railway was rebuilt as a 2ft gauge 3rd-rail electric (250v DC) passenger railway. A mere 700yd long, it carries some 650,000 passengers a year.

2

Light railways

The Light Railways Bill went through Parliament in 1896. It had long been the wish of Parliamentarians and others to find a cheaper way of authorising railways to enable them to be used to open up 'remote areas'. A clause in the 1868 Regulation of Railways Act had gone some way towards this, but reluctance on the part of the Board of Trade to allow it to be used as intended meant that it was rarely used. The Light Railways Act gave Parliamentary status to railways using a non-Parliamentary process; railways thus authorised were subject to restrictions on axle weights, which had the effect of limiting speed. Although the Act placed no universal restriction on speed, some orders did restrict speeds on the railways concerned; the 1868 Act's 25mph speed limit for light railways is often erroneously attributed to the 1896 Act.

What might be called traditional narrow gauge light railways were the Welshpool & Llanfair, Leek & Manifold, Campbeltown & Machrihanish, Sand Hutton, Welsh Highland, Romney, Hythe & Dymchurch and Ashover lines. The Vale of Rheidol and Festiniog Railways were brought within the Act's remit in 1902 and 1923 respectively. After 1960 the Light Railways Act was used to transfer British Rail assets to organisations intending to create and operate railways as tourist attractions. Narrow gauge railways thus created were the Brecon Mountain, Welsh Highland (Porthmadog), Bala Lake, Wells & Walsingham, Launceston Steam, Teifi Valley, Bure Valley and Welsh Highland (Caernarfon-Dinas) Railways, and the Kirklees Light Railway. A 15-inch-gauge railway constructed at the former Steamtown Railway Centre, Carnforth, was authorised by a Light Railway Order that covered the entire site.

The first two lines drew on the light railway philosophy developed by the engineer E. R. Calthrop and were of 2ft 6in gauge. His ideas were showcased on the Indian Barsi Light Railway, opened in 1897 and described in a paper published the same year. He argued that this gauge was the best compromise between economy of construction and capacity. It also became popular with the Ministry of Defence,

and in industry it was used at the Bowater paper mill at Sittingbourne, Kent. As 750mm it was widely used overseas. Both the Welshpool & Llanfair and Leek & Manifold light railways were partially financed with Treasury and local authority loans, to qualify for which the railways had to be built and operated by existing railway companies.

❧

Fifty miles to the east of Aberystwyth and 20 miles west of Shrewsbury, the **Welshpool & Llanfair Light Railway** was built and operated by the Cambrian Railways. It was the first narrow gauge railway to be built using powers obtained under the Light Railways Act.

The Light Railway Order made in 1899 had taken more than two years to obtain, and a second was required to increase capital before construction started. The line was opened for goods on 9 March 1903 and to passengers on 6 April. It ran 9 miles westwards from a terminus opposite the Cambrian's station at Welshpool, terminating on the edge of the rural community of Llanfair Caereinion. Unlike the other Welsh narrow gauge lines, the imperative to build it came from agriculture rather than the prospect of mineral traffic.

At Welshpool the line forged a sinuous route through the town, straddling the Lledan brook and crossing several roads before reaching open countryside at Raven Square. Notable features are the climb to Golfa, which includes a section of 1 in 29, the steepest on any British public railway, a stone viaduct at Brynelin and the Banwy river bridge at Heniarth.

Beyer, Peacock supplied two sturdy 0-6-0T locomotives, and three bogie carriages with longitudinal seats were obtained from R. Y. Pickering. Most trains ran mixed.

At opening, the railway was both undercapitalised and overspent. The contractor's claim for £20,000 for extras went to arbitration, taking three years to resolve before it was settled for £5,413. The

railway was never debt-free, owing £2,387 to the Cambrian by 31 December 1922. At the railway Grouping in 1923, the GWR paid £20,000 for the railway and took on the debt.

The GWR rebuilt the locomotives at Swindon and withdrew the passenger service in 1931, the carriages being scrapped. British Railways obtained approval to close the railway in 1950, but ran it until 1956. Several 'farewell' excursions were run with passengers riding in the coal wagons. Following the examples of the Talyllyn and Ffestiniog lines, a preservation society was formed, taking over the railway, except the town section, by means of a Light Railway Transfer Order in 1963. The local authorities were insistent that the level crossings on the town section should be closed and would not agree to the line there being reopened.

The 60th anniversary of the opening was marked by the restoration of services between Llanfair Caereinion and Castle Caereinion. The original locomotives had been bought from BR and carriages obtained from the Admiralty. The first years were difficult, especially after the

ABOVE Photographed at Llanfair Caereinion shortly after the Welshpool & Llanfair Light Railway had been opened in 1903, Beyer, Peacock 0-6-0T *The Earl* has just arrived from Welshpool with a short mixed train.

Banwy bridge was undermined by scouring in December 1964, but gradually the railway found its feet, extending back to Castle Caereinion in 1965, to Sylfaen in 1972, and to Raven Square, on the edge of Welshpool, in 1981.

For additional locomotives and rolling stock the line looked overseas, acquiring locomotives from Austria, Antigua, Sierra Leone, Finland and Romania, and carriages from Austria, Sierra Leone and Hungary, all of which give the railway a very distinctive appearance. Passengers particularly enjoy riding on the carriage balconies.

A Lottery-supported project included the reboilering of the original locomotives in time for their centenary in 2003. Partially funded by a benefactor, three replica Pickering carriages built by the Ffestiniog Railway were delivered between 2005 and 2010.

LEFT Everyone stops for the camera! *The Earl* poses at Llanfair Caereinion shortly after the Welshpool & Llanfair Light Railway was opened.

RIGHT Welshpool & Llanfair Light Railway 0-6-0T *The Countess* stands at Llanfair Caereinion. The cabside plate identifies the locomotive as No 2 in the light railway's fleet. Although the railway was operated by the Cambrian Railways, the locomotives belonged to the narrow gauge company.

THE LLANFAIR RAILWAY, GLYN GOLFA, WELSHPOOL

LEFT In about 1904 a mixed train arrives at Golfa, the climb from Welshpool including a section at 1 in 29, the steepest on a British passenger railway. *Valentine*

LEFT When the Great Western Railway took over the light railway a number of changes were wrought on the locomotives; No 2 *The Countess* became No 823 *Countess* and both receiving standard Swindon fittings when they were reboilered. There is no doubt about the owner's identity in this photograph. The locomotive shed is behind the second carriage, with the carriage shed alongside. A mirror image of this arrangement has been created at Raven Square.

ABOVE This fine portrait of *Countess* was probably taken on 2 July 1949, when the Birmingham Locomotive Club ran the first passenger train over the line since 1931. The letter 'W' painted under the number plate denotes the locomotive's attachment to the Western Region of British Railways.

BELOW The route past Seven Stars is seen on 15 September 1956. Inconsiderate car parking and increased traffic contributed to the local authorities' apathy towards the rail route through Welshpool and their desire to seen it removed. Nowadays they would see it as a benefit, attracting tourists. *E. K. Stretch*

ABOVE During the 1950s local BR management became quite accommodating to enthusiasts wishing to experience narrow gauge goods trains. On 31 March 1963 the train is starting away from the Llanfair water tank, which remained in use until 1979. Installation of the tank is surrounded by a degree of mystery, an unusual rivet line prompting speculation that it might have its origins in a broad gauge locomotive tender.

BELOW Towards the end, the locomotives had been smartened up with some paint on their number plates and their nameplates had been removed to protect them from souvenir hunters. No 822 is crossing Church Street.

RIGHT With a headboard mounted, *The Earl* climbs the Golfa bank with the Stephenson Locomotive Society's special train on 3 November 1956.

BELOW An excursion on 6 October 1962 was photographed approaching Raven Square. The train included three of the four 'toast-rack' carriages obtained from the Admiralty's Chattenden & Upnor Railway. The larger vehicle at the rear, the combination car, came from the same source; it is now used as a mess car on the Welsh Highland Railway. Banking the train is the former Lodge Hill & Upnor Railway's Planet, *Upnor Castle*, which was sold to the Festiniog Railway in 1968. The 'toast-racks' were sold to the Sittingbourne & Kemsley Light Railway in 1978.

LEFT In 1963 the preservation company ran services between Llanfair Caereinion and Castle Caereinion, 4½ miles. From 6 June 1964 services were run to Sylfaen, another mile towards Welshpool. The extra track deteriorated so quickly that services were cut back to Castle Caereinion before the end of the season. The lack of a loop required the diesel locomotive to shunt the stock and release *The Countess* for the return journey. It was 1972 before services were resumed to the roadside station. A loop was provided in 1976.

ABOVE The Admiralty carriages could only be a stopgap measure – they were open to the elements and unsuitable for equipping with vacuum brakes. Their replacements were donated by the Zillertalbahn in Austria, four in 1968 and one in 1975, and their balconies made them an immediate success with the travelling public. The second carriage had just arrived when this photograph was taken in the autumn of 1975. *Author*

BELOW In 1904 one of the piers of the Banwy river bridge was found to have been undermined by scouring. Sixty years later the same thing happened again, nearly bringing the company to its knees. On this occasion the repair was carried out by the Royal Engineers as a military exercise and the line was reopened after eight months.

Problems with the bridge recurred in 1997, with the discovery of corrosion and scouring, and it took until 1999 to find and implement an effective solution. Seen on 15 June 2003, the locomotive is Tubize 2-6-2T *Orion*. Built in Belgium in 1948 for the Jokioistenrautatie in Finland, it was bought by an English enthusiast in 1972 and sold to the WLLR in 1983. After an overhaul it entered service in 2000 but, despite its size, it was not really suitable for the WLLR's varied gradients, being designed for relatively high speeds on a reasonably flat line. In 2006 it was sold to the Jokionen Museum Railway in Finland. *Author*

ABOVE Apart from the Banwy river bridge, the WLLR's main engineering feature is the six-arch Brynelin Viaduct near Cyfronydd. This once attractive photographic vantage point is now severely restricted by tree growth. *Author*

BELOW When the railway was restored to Raven Square, Welshpool, in 1981 there was still a great deal of work outstanding on the station, as this photograph taken on 21 August demonstrates. The 1954-built Hunslet 2-6-2T had been imported from Sierra Leone in 1975 with four carriages built by the Gloucester Railway Carriage & Wagon Company. *Author*

ABOVE With the aid of a Lottery grant and a successful appeal to members, both of the WLLR's original locomotives were rebuilt with new boilers in time for the railway's centenary. The first time they appeared together in steam was on 3 June 2002. *Author*

BELOW Four of the WLLR's intermediate stations – Golfa, Castle Caereinion, Cyfronydd and Heniarth – were equipped with loops that were actually double-ended sidings, arranged to facilitate shunting wagons on and off trains regardless of the direction of travel. To accommodate timber trains, Castle Caereinion was signalled to enable trains to cross in 1907, but two years later the light railway directors discovered that the facility had hardly been used. Now the loop is used on just a few days each year. The ex-Sierra Leone Hunslet 2-6-2T was photographed in 1999. *Author*

RIGHT In the name of safety, the sight of a WLLR fireman disembarking to flag his/her train across the Dolarddyn level crossing will soon be a thing of the past. Elizabeth Hall performs this duty on 1 September 2012. *Author*

RIGHT A relic of the past is the bridge that once carried the Llanfair trains across the Shropshire Union Canal. Recently refurbished, it was photographed on 14 May 2011 at 6.48am; it is only illuminated by the sun early in the morning, and the photographer's presence at this time was coincidental. *Author*

BELOW If anyone had dared to suggest, when the railway's revival was first started in 1963, that within 50 years it would have a rake of Pickering carriages, the idea would have been dismissed as preposterous! 31 August 2013. *Author*

River Manifold, near Thor's Cave. North Stafford. Railway.

In a remote area of North Staffordshire, the **Leek & Manifold Light Railway** ran between Waterhouses and Hulme End, a distance of 8½ miles, operated by the North Staffordshire Railway.

After two years of planning, in 1899 the relevant Light Railway Order authorised two railways, a standard gauge branch of the North Staffordshire Railway from Cheddleton, near Leek, to Waterhouses, 9¾ miles, and its narrow gauge continuation into the Manifold valley. The latter was to be financed and maintained by the Leek & Manifold Valley Light Railway Company.

Construction was started in 1902, taking just over two years. Calthrop's principles required all vehicles, including locomotives, to have the same axle loading to permit the maximum loading of goods wagons, 5 tons allowing the use of rails weighing 30lb per yard.

Calthrop's influence was demonstrated in the design of the two Kitson 2-6-4T locomotives and the four gangwayed open saloon carriages with open balconies built in Preston. Most stations had a short length of standard gauge track to accommodate vehicles carried on transporter wagons. The locomotives were painted brown and the carriages primrose yellow.

The line meandered through the Manifold valley, a popular tourist destination that brought the railway most of its passengers, the local communities being thinly spread. Simply, the gradient profile was V-shaped, the line falling to Grindon from either end. The steepest section was a short 1 in 40 near Waterhouses. The tunnel at Swainley, near Hulme End, is 164 yards long.

ABOVE This classic view of the Leek & Manifold Valley Light Railway epitomises everything there is to say about the railway and its surroundings. *North Staffordshire Railway*

The North Staffordshire Railway did much to publicise the Manifold valley and its railway, commissioning photographs and publishing several coloured picture postcards to promote them. At bank holidays traffic was so heavy that every vehicle was pressed into use, passengers even riding on the transporter wagons.

The main traffic, however, was milk, which increased substantially when a new dairy was opened at Ecton, 7¼ miles from Waterhouses, in 1918. Its closure in 1932 precipitated the railway's own closure the following year. In common with the Welshpool & Llanfair Light Railway, the LMVLR was saddled with construction debt that it was unable to pay off. At the railway Grouping in 1923 the London Midland & Scottish Railway had acquired the line for just short of £30,000, less than half of its £68,000 capital expenditure. There was little incentive to keep the railway open once the main traffic had gone.

The line was demolished in 1937 and its trackbed donated to Staffordshire County Council. As it was cleared it was converted into a footpath that is now called the Manifold Way. Motor vehicles were given access to a 2-mile section, including the tunnel, in 1952. The Hulme End station building was restored as a visitor centre in 1997 and Waterhouses signal box is preserved at the Amerton Railway near Uttoxeter.

ABOVE No 2 *J. B. Earle* stands with three carriages at Wetton Mill in 1907. The photograph was commissioned by the North Staffordshire Railway for LMVLR promotional purposes. *Edwin Harrison*

BELOW No 1 *E. R. Calthrop* with a mixed train that includes two empty standard gauge wagons crosses the river at Redhurst. The pony and cart on the left are at the churn loading platform. The LMVLR directors obviously had a high opinion of their engineers, to name both of their locomotives after them.

ABOVE Thor's Cave, 5 miles from Waterhouses, featured in many postcards and photographs of the LMVLR.

BELOW This postcard gives an impression of the restricted site on which the exchange station at Waterhouses was located. The narrow gauge train, mostly obscured by the shelter, includes a loaded transporter wagon. The presence of a North Staffordshire Railway inspection saloon, ladders and a trestle on the ground, and a photographer, indicates that the photograph was taken just before the station was opened on 1 July 1905.

ABOVE Two wagons loaded with milk bound for London are pulled out of the Ecton dairy by 2-6-4T No 1 *E. R. Calthrop* in the 1930s. The spoil heaps are from a worked-out copper mine, once claimed to be the most profitable in Britain.

LEFT The LMVLR's ornate liveries lost favour with the London Midland & Scottish Railway after 1923, both locomotives and carriages being painted in crimson lake as seen at Hulme End on 29 April 1930. The locomotive shed is on the right. *H. C. Casserley*

LEFT After the railway was closed in 1934 2-6-4T No 1 *E. R. Calthrop* and the transporter wagons remained on the line until track lifting was started in 1937, when No 1 was steamed by the contractor to haul the demolition trains. The hose draped over the locomotive enabled water to be taken from any convenient flowing water. It will never be known who thought it was a good idea to fly the Union flag.

ON BOARD TURBINE S. S. QUEEN ALEXANDRA

ROGER. Photo. Campbeltown.

TURBINE EXPRESS
CAMPBELTOWN TO MACHRIHANISH

The coalfield on the Mull of Kintyre, on Scotland's Argyll coast, is virtually unknown nowadays, but the 2ft 3in-gauge railway developed to serve it from 1877 became Scotland's only public narrow gauge railway, the **Campbeltown & Machrihanish Light Railway**. The railway ran east-west across the Kintyre peninsula for about 5 miles and had two steam locomotives.

Although some coal was exported, most was consumed locally, so demand for it was seasonal. As Campbeltown was a popular tourist destination for visitors travelling by ferry from Glasgow, the colliery company registered the Argyll Railway Company and obtained a Light Railway Order in 1905.

The mineral railway was rebuilt with modifications in some places that made it slightly more than 5 miles long. At Campbeltown it ran as a street tramway onto the wharf. The train service started in August 1906, just in time for the tourists.

Two of the colliery locomotives were retained to deal with the coal traffic, one of them having vacuum brakes fitted to enable its use with light passenger trains. Two handsome Barclay 0-6-2Ts were bought for the ordinary passenger service, and Pickering supplied six 43-foot-long bogie carriages, larger versions of those previously supplied to the Welshpool & Llanfair Light Railway.

In common with most of the other railways accounted for here, the CMLR was a victim of the inter-war depression and competition from motor transport. There was no joy to be had from the operation of two motor buses purchased to augment the train service, and in 1932 the want of repairs to the steam locomotives brought an end to the railway. A winding-up order was obtained in November 1933 and the railway was dismantled by a scrap merchant in 1934.

ABOVE The Barclay 0-6-2Ts of the Campbeltown & Machrihanish Light Railway must have been the largest locomotives built on the 2ft 3in gauge. *Atlantic* covers Campbeltown with smoke as it departs for Machrihanish.
Roger/Campbeltown

RIGHT In this fine portrait of *Atlantic* on the quay at Campbeltown in later years, the lettering of its painted name has nearly faded away.

CAMPBELTOWN AND MACHRIHANISH LIGHT RAILWAY.

FIRST CAR THROUGH RURAL DISTRICT.

Tram Conductor (rustic): "Here, ladies and gentlemen, there's something wrong with my 'Fare Bill,' you'll ALL have to pay again!"

ABOVE *Argyll* and its train await the right away at Machrihanish in 1906. It is a wonder that Lieutenant Colonel Druitt had nothing to say about the platform here when he made his inspection. With their open balconies and lattice gates, the carriages were not dissimilar to those Pickering had supplied to the Welshpool & Llanfair Light Railway. The distant mast was part of the transatlantic telegraph installation.

LEFT A light-hearted view on the impact made by the light railway when it opened in 1906.
Will Hall/Martin

The **Sand Hutton Light Railway** Order was made in 1920. Opened in 1922/23 and 5½ miles long, the railway was an 18-inch-gauge estate line developed by Sir Robert Walker Bt. In serving the Sand Hutton estate it made a connection with the North Eastern Railway's York-Beverley line at Warthill. When construction had started it had been 15-inch gauge like Sir Robert's earlier 1½-mile-long leisure line that he had completed in 1914, but the availability of government-surplus 18-inch-gauge equipment prompted a change of gauge. The railway covered its costs until 1930 and was closed in 1932.

ABOVE Sir Robert Walker is at the controls of his 15-inch-gauge Bassett-Lowke 4-4-2 at Sand Hutton. He named the locomotive *Synolda*, after his first wife. It is preserved in working order in the Ravenglass & Eskdale Railway's museum.

BELOW Three of these 18-inch-gauge Hunslet 0-4-0WTs were obtained from the Deptford Special Reserve Depot for the Sand Hutton Light Railway in 1921 and a fourth was obtained via an agent in 1927. Twelve had been built for use in the depot in 1917. Seen at Warthill on 23 July 1927, the front buffer beam of No 12 had been damaged in a collision with a tree stump. *Humphrey Household*

LEFT The SHLR's passenger carriage and brake van were supplied by the Leeds firm of Robert Hudson Ltd. The carriage is preserved in the Lincolnshire Coast Light Railway's collection near Skegness. *Humphrey Household*

ABOVE The level crossing on Porthmadog's Britannia bridge is just one of the many features that distinguish the restored Welsh Highland Railway from other railways, regardless of gauge. No 87 attracts a small crowd with the last arrival on 5 August 2011. *Author*

Opened between Dinas, 3 miles from Caernarfon, and Porthmadog in 1923, the **Welsh Highland Railway** has a long and complex history that, in its reincarnated form, includes part of one of the oldest Welsh narrow gauge railways, the 3ft 6in-gauge Nantlle Railway.

Its story starts with the North Wales Narrow Gauge Railways' Moel Tryfan undertaking, a 2-foot-gauge line that made an interchange with the London & North Western Railway at Dinas. Empowered by an 1872 Act of Parliament, it had a 9-mile main line to Rhyd Ddu, serving quarries and small communities, opened in stages between 1877 and 1881, and a 2-mile branch from Tryfan Junction to Bryngwyn, opened in 1877, where a railway-owned incline connected it to several slate quarries.

Based on a survey made by Charles Easton Spooner, the railway was built cheaply, following the contours where possible and having gradients as steep as 1 in 40. At Rhyd Ddu the station was the closest to the summit of Snowdon.

The delay between obtaining the Act and completing the line is indicative of the problems encountered. There was a dispute with the contractor and the financier put the company into receivership in 1877. A shareholder who had agreed to lease the line in 1873 repudiated on the agreement when it was ready to be opened.

Two single Fairlies obtained from Vulcan Foundry in 1875 were a consequence of the 1873 lease, which called for Fairlie patent locomotives to be used on ordinary trains. A third, non-articulated, locomotive was obtained for the Bryngwyn branch in 1878.

The railway company being unable to meet its obligations to pay for the rolling stock, one of the shareholders bought it and transferred it to a company formed for the purpose later in 1878. Suing for non-payment, the rolling stock company put the railway back into receivership just a few months after it had been released from the financier's receivership.

This set the tone for the NWNGR, which remained in receivership for the rest of its existence. Merchants soon discovered that they were

better off sending their goods by road because transhipment with the LNWR at Dinas took 24 hours. A brainwave to rename Rhyd Ddu station Snowdon in 1893 brought an increase in the number of tourists carried, which lasted only until the Snowdon Mountain Railway opened in 1895.

The Portmadoc, Beddgelert & South Snowdon Railway might have brought modernisation, in the form of electrification, to the NWNGR had its sponsors, the North Wales Power & Traction Company, not run short of funds. The PBSSR was intended to be a 2-foot-gauge electric railway from Borth y Gest via Portmadoc and Beddgelert to Nant Gwynant, where it would serve a new hydro-electric power station, in turn the source of its power. Between Portmadoc and the later Croesor Junction it intended to use the horse-worked Croesor Tramway, opened in 1864 and acquired by the PBSSR.

Including the NWNGR in its plans, the PBSSR said that it would electrify and work it and make a connecting railway between Rhyd Ddu and its own line at Beddgelert. Construction was started around Beddgelert in 1905 but ended in 1906, when available funds were needed to complete the power station.

The NWNGR did benefit from the PBSSR activity in that it was given a Hunslet 2-6-2T to replace the worn-out 1878 locomotive. It was otherwise in a poor state that was only slightly improved when its reserves were used to buy two carriages in 1907 and another Fairlie locomotive in 1908.

By the time war broke out in 1914 there were very few passengers, and goods traffic was worked as required. In 1917 the least-worn parts of the 1875 Fairlie locomotives were used to make one good loco. The 1908 locomotive was sold to the Ministry of Munitions around this time.

ABOVE The most substantial part of the revived Welsh Highland Railway was the North Wales Narrow Gauge Railways, which carried slate from quarries on Moel Tryfan and along the Gwrfai valley to Dinas to be forwarded to Caernarfon, 3 miles away. Two 0-6-4T single Fairlies built by Vulcan Foundry in 1874 were named *Snowdon Ranger* and *Moel Tryfan*. The latter is seen here waiting to return to Dinas from Rhyd Ddu. When the station was renamed Snowdon in 1893 the traffic it attracted away from Llanberis was the catalyst for the development of the Snowdon Mountain Railway. The third carriage in the train is mounted on a six-wheeled Cleminson underframe.

In 1914 the local authorities decided to take action by making a Light Railway Order application for powers to take over the NWNGR and the PBSSR, to complete the railway between Porthmadog and Dinas, and to transfer the powers to a private company to undertake the works and operate the railway. The war immediately put the application on hold.

It was reactivated in 1919, after the Aluminium Corporation at Dolgarrog had acquired the North Wales Power Company and with it the PBSSR. The moribund NWNGR was acquired by the PBSSR and applications were made for £75,000 loans to pay for the assets, completing the PBSSR, refurbishing the NWNGR and making the Croesor section of the PBSSR suitable for locomotive working.

With loan funding from the Ministry of Transport and the local authorities, the Light Railway Order was made in 1922 and the refurbished NWNGR was reopened as the Welsh Highland Railway. A second LRO was made in 1923 to make the gradients around Beddgelert suitable for steam working. The WHR promoters took over the Festiniog Railway and obtained an order enabling it to build junction railways connecting the railways at Portmadoc and to build a new station there. The WHR was opened through to Portmadoc in June 1923.

Thanks to advertising on the North Wales coast, 1923 turned out to be the WHR's best year. However, neither passenger nor mineral traffic came anywhere near the promoters' expectations. The railway was affected by improvements to the roads and visitors who preferred modern charabancs to rickety old steam trains. It became known for late running and lengthy journey times. In 1927 Carnarvonshire County Council put the railway into receivership to protect the investing authorities' interests when a creditor obtained a judgment in its favour.

The county council's proposal that the railway should not be reopened in 1934 prompted the FR to lease the WHR, but it was no more successful and gave up after three seasons. In 1941 the investing authorities agreed to the WHR being requisitioned for the war effort and the FR was released from the lease.

Unusually, the WHR company was still in liquidation when a society was formed to restore it in 1961. The liquidator offered to sell the trackbed for £750, but no sale had been concluded by the time he died in 1964, shortly after the society had formed a company to take the project forward.

This company established a base on land bought from British Rail adjacent to the WHR at Porthmadog in 1973 and built a railway on it that was opened in 1980. It was given and restored the Hunslet 2-6-2T *Russell*, the only surviving locomotive owned by the original company, and created a heritage train that incorporated original vehicles sold for alternative uses in 1941. While dealing with the Official Receiver and the local authorities proved not to be very fruitful, the company's activities did protect the trackbed from incursion.

During the 1980s the FR became interested in the WHR, concerned about a competitor being established in Porthmadog. Amidst controversy and scepticism, it declared that it would restore the WHR in full, including the connection at Porthmadog and extending it over the Carnarvonshire Railway route to Caernarfon.

By 1999, when the Transport & Works Order was made sanctioning the WHR's reconstruction, the issue had been aired in the High Court and at three public enquiries. In the meantime a funding boost had been obtained in 1995, when the Lottery-funded Millennium Commission announced that it would contribute £4.3 million towards the cost of building the line between Caernarfon and Rhyd Ddu.

Empowered by the Caernarfon Light Railway Order, the first section was opened between Dinas and Caernarfon in 1997. This had its origins in the Nantlle Railway, which was opened in 1828. Taken over by the Carnarvonshire Railway, the section between Penygroes and Caernarfon was rebuilt to form part of the line to Afon Wen, which opened in 1867.

For the new WHR, locomotives and much other equipment had been obtained from South Africa, and carriages were purpose-built. After the delay in obtaining powers, the line to Waunfawr was opened in 2000. Opening to Rhyd Ddu was delayed until 2003 by the foot & mouth disease outbreak.

Construction onwards to Porthmadog was started in 2005, aided by a £5 million grant from the Welsh Government, some substantial donations and £2 million raised by a very successful public appeal. Services to Beddgelert and Hafod y Llyn started in 2009 and to Pont Croesor in 2010. Some trains were extended to Porthmadog in 2011 and a full service was operated over the line from 2012.

To accommodate the WHR at Porthmadog a programme to widen Madocks's embankment to make space for platforms was started in 2012. Completed in 2014, the final layout is fully signalled from a new McKenzie & Holland-style signal box.

ABOVE Hunslet 2-6-2T *Russell* was 'donated' to the NWNGR by the North Wales Power Company, via its subsidiary, the Portmadoc, Beddgelert & South Snowdon Railway, in 1906. The power company was developing the hydro-electric power station in Nant Gwynant and the proposed electric railway would both use power and provide routes for the transmission lines. It was intended that the NWNGR should be a part of the network and electrified, but the power company ran short of funds and devoted its

attentions on the power station. Russell was the name of the NWNGR's chairman and receiver. In service, the locomotive replaced the 1878-built Hunslet 0-6-4T *Beddgelert*, which was withdrawn the same year having been worn out working the Bryngwyn traffic.

BELOW In 1922, when this photograph was taken at Rhyd Ddu, the NWNGR had been refurbished and reopened as a part of the Welsh Highland Railway.

LEFT Before the PBSSR scheme was abandoned in 1906, substantial works had been carried out around Beddgelert, including this embankment at Nantmor and the tunnels in the Aberglaslyn Pass.

RIGHT The McAlpine family refurbished the NWNGR, completed the PBSSR and made the Croesor Tramway between Porthmadog and Croesor Junction suitable for steam traction. Part of the PBSSR alignment was also altered to accommodate steam haulage instead of electric traction. The bridge at Bryn y Felin was one of three of this type installed between Beddgelert and Croesor Junction.

RIGHT The Welsh Highland promoters, who had also taken control of the Festiniog Railway, intended the stock to be capable of working on both railways, but the former NWNGR equipment required alteration before it could be run on the FR. This photograph shows *Russell* and NWNGR carriages at Beddgelert in their original condition.

ABOVE *Russell* was altered in 1924; the result was not very elegant, and the locomotive was still unable to pass through the FR's low structures. The photograph dates from the FR lease period and shows one of the WHR's innovations, the narrow gauge railway buffet car. Two four-wheeled vans have been attached to the train, which is heading for Dinas.

BELOW In 1923 a series of publicity photographs were taken using an FR train hauled by that railway's 0-4-0STT *Palmerston*. This was something of a return visit for the locomotive, for it had been hired to the contractor working on the railway in 1877 and in 1923.

ABOVE At Porthmadog (then known as Portmadoc), the FR's resources were used to provide a new joint station close to the Cambrian line from Barmouth to Pwllheli. The buildings on the left included a tearoom run by the Snowdon Mountain Railway, which was also controlled by the WHR promoters.

BELOW The Festiniog Railway was responsible for the junction lines that connected the two railways and for a time all of the FR's trains worked through to the new station.

ABOVE The passage of trains past Beddgelert and through the Aberglaslyn Pass was as popular with photographers then as it is now. *Russell* is seen at Bryn y Felin not long after the railway was opened. *Frith*

LEFT When the track was lifted in 1941 the larger structures were left in situ to enable the railway to be reopened in better times. When it came to it, the three bridges installed by the McAlpines were unsuitable, both by design and lack of maintenance. Their replacements look almost the identical.

LEFT *Russell* returned to Wales after an axle broke when it was working in Dorset in 1955. Purchased by the Birmingham Locomotive Club in 1955, it was displayed at the Talyllyn Railway until 1965, when it was donated to Welsh Highland Light Railway (1964) Limited.

LEFT Under the auspices of the company formed in 1964, trains started running under the Welsh Highland Railway name on the Beddgelert siding in Porthmadog in 1980. This scene at Pen y Mount dates from 1982. *Author*

RIGHT The company was given the only surviving locomotive owned by the original Welsh Highland Railway, Hunslet 2-6-2T *Russell*, in 1965 and returned it to service with a new Hunslet boiler in 1987. During a second overhaul completed in 2014 North Wales Narrow Gauge Railways' features and livery were restored. The loco was captured running round its train at Pen y Mount whilst working its first public post-overhaul train on 2 August 2014. The railway now operates as the Welsh Highland Heritage Railway. *Author*

RIGHT Services on the revived Welsh Highland Railway started between Dinas and Caernarfon, on a formation that had been built by the contractor Thomas Savin for the Carnarvonshire Railway, and which in turn incorporated parts of the 3ft 6in-gauge Nantlle Railway. Garratt No 138 is about to cross the Seiont viaduct, just outside Caernarfon, on 25 October 1997. *Author*

ABOVE As the railway was extended towards Porthmadog, the trains got progressively longer, with ten cars becoming the norm. This view of No 138 and six cars approaching Rhyd Ddu shows some of the curves that are a feature of this area. *Author*

BELOW Ffestiniog Railway locomotives and carriages are often to be seen on the WHR now the railways are connected. When this photograph was taken at Tryfan Junction, however, *Prince* and its train had made the journey by road. The derelict station building has since been restored by the Welsh Highland Railway Heritage Group. In a community initiative supported by the railway company, the trackbed of the Bryngwyn branch is being developed as a footpath. *Author*

TOP LEFT Small train, big scenery. Garratt No 87 passes the site of the Glan yr afon quarry sidings, between Snowdon Ranger and Rhyd Ddu, on 5 July 2013. The observation car, *Glaslyn*, which brings up the rear, was named by HM the Queen on 27 April 2010. *Author*

BOTTOM LEFT Emerging from the Aberglaslyn Pass on 18 July 2013, Garratt No 143 and its train traverse an embankment constructed by the abortive Portmadoc, Beddgelert & South Snowdon Railway more than a century before. The Pullman car was sponsored by the Bodysgallen Country House Hotel, near Llandudno. *Author*

TOP RIGHT Cnicht (left) and the Moelwyns provide the backdrop for Garratt No 138 at Pont Croesor on 18 July 2013. The route here was originally a part of the Croesor Tramway, built in 1864. *Author*

CENTRE RIGHT Another view of No 87, crossing the Britannia bridge at Porthmadog on 20 May 2012. *Author*

BOTTOM RIGHT A feature of railway events developed strongly in the 21st century is the concept of visiting locomotives. In 2014 the Statfold Barn Railway's newly restored Hudswell, Clarke 0-6-0, built for use on a Fijian sugar estate in 1912, visited the Welsh Highland Railway for the season. Displaying its spark-arresting chimney and double-skinned cab roof, it was photographed piloting Garratt No 143 at Plas y Nant on 19 April, the first time it had been used on a WHR passenger train. *Author*

The Light Railway, Ashover.

The last of the 'classic' British narrow gauge railways was the 2-foot-gauge **Ashover Light Railway**. Developed by the Clay Cross Company in Derbyshire, it also demonstrated the economic advantages of narrow gauge.

The company had been established by George Stephenson when coal was found during the course of building the North Midland Railway between Derby and Leeds in 1837. The colliery was followed by the development of coke ovens, lime works, brick works and blast furnaces. In pursuit of other minerals at Fallgate, in 1919 the company obtained a Light Railway Order authorising the construction of a standard gauge railway 4 miles long between Stretton, on the Midland Railway, and Ashover. The estimates, however, deterred the company from proceeding until the consulting engineer, Colonel Holman Fred Stephens, suggested making it a narrow gauge line, which made the scheme affordable.

A second order in 1922 changed the gauge of the authorised railway and added a 2-mile extension from Stretton to Clay Cross, and a third in 1924 extended it to the quarry at Ashover Butts, which also made a more convenient terminus. The line, 7¼ miles long, was opened for goods in 1924 and for passengers in 1925. The steepest gradient was a section of 1 in 37 on the climb to the summit half a mile from Clay Cross. Then the line fell steadily for 3 miles before climbing to Ashover, claimed to be 'the remotest town in mid-Derbyshire'.

Motive power was five ex-War Department Baldwin 4-6-0PTs, the same type as that already encountered on the Welsh Highland Railway; four locomotives had been obtained initially but when one of them was found to be in poor condition it was cheaper to replace it with two more locomotives than to repair it. A petrol-electric locomotive put into service as a shunter in 1928 was replaced by a diesel-electric locomotive in 1939.

Four bogie carriages supplied by the Gloucester Railway Carriage & Wagon Company were joined by eight others that had been used at

ABOVE Children playing in the River Amber ignore one of the Ashover Light Railway's Baldwin 4-6-0PTs waiting to return to Clay Cross in 1927. The left-hand carriage was one of those that ran at the Wembley exhibition. Triangles at each end of the line enabled trains to operate with their locomotives running chimney-first in each direction. The track to the left ran to the Butt's quarry, that in the centre to the station and coal siding. The railway-owned café, whimsically named 'Where the Rainbow Ends', stands on the hillside. *R. Sneath*

the British Empire Exhibition at Wembley in 1924/25 for use at bank holidays, when the line was promoted as 'the little railway'. At Ashover the railway ran the winsomely-named 'Where the Rainbow Ends' café.

The inter-war depression and competition from motor transport eventually caught up with the Ashover Light Railway, the passenger service becoming seasonal from September 1933 and being withdrawn completely in 1936. The final passenger train was run in 1947, when members of three railway societies rode in open wagons.

Although in decline, the mineral service continued until the railway was closed in 1950. The steam locomotives still in traffic were in poor condition, so to keep it going a Planet diesel had been purchased in 1948.

Dismantling was completed in September 1951, when the Planet was the only locomotives to survive; named *Ashover*, it is now preserved on the Ffestiniog Railway. The carriages did better: the Gloucester vehicles were found other uses by the Clay Cross Company until two of them were acquired by the Lincolnshire Coast Light Railway in 1961. Another was used as a clubhouse at the Clay Cross bowling green from 1953 until 2007, when it was acquired by the Golden Valley Light Railway at Butterley, Derbyshire, where it is being restored. Some track and wagons continued in use for the extraction of fluorspar at Fallgate until 1968.

A society formed in 2007 to preserve relics of the railway wants to restore a 2½-mile section of it.

RIGHT Located on the edge of the village, the Ashover Light Railway's passenger terminus at Ashover was overlooked by Butts Methodist chapel. Here, children amuse themselves on the hillside as a train arrives from Clay Cross and a loaded bogie wagon awaits the attention of the coal merchant. The carriage is on the bridge carrying the line over the Marsh brook. The ice cream stall behind the basic station building, typical of light railways, did not survive the opening of the railway's own café in 1926.
Clay Cross Company

Terminus of Ashover Light Railway at The Butts, Ashover.

LEFT Seen amongst the industrial detritus at Clay Cross, *Joan* was one of six ex-War Department Baldwin 4-6-0PTs owned by the Ashover Light Railway. They were named after the children of the railway's chairman, Brigadier-General Geoffrey Meinertzhagen Jackson. He had been a Clay Cross Company director since 1891 and was chairman and managing director from 1930 until 1946.

LEFT One of the ALR's wayside halts was Chesterfield Road, on the edge of Clay Cross. The railway crossed the road by a bridge just beyond the building.

LEFT Six miles from Clay Cross, the photographer called this Mill Town, but the railway called it Fallgate, the source of most of the company's traffic. *R. Sneath*

ABOVE On 24 August 1947, nearly 11 years after the last passenger trains had been run, an excursion was operated for the Birmingham Locomotive Club, with members riding in the wagons. *Joan* was the last steam locomotive in traffic.

RIGHT Part of the railway continued in use to transport fluorspar at Fallgate until 1968/69. This view of a loaded wagon must have been taken not long before the end.

3

Industrial railways

Even now most people would be unacquainted with the use of railways of any gauge in industry. No special authority was required to build a railway on private property. Where required, arrangements for level crossings were made with the local authorities concerned and Acts of Parliament or Light Railway Orders were rarely required or obtained. Industrial uses of railways, particularly narrow gauge, were many and varied. The extractive industries – slate, granite, coal, clay, iron ore and peat – were big users and many sites used steam locomotives. Until they were overcome by the development of reliable motor vehicles, construction projects were invariably accompanied by temporary railways for the transportation of spoil and materials. In manufacturing, the paper mills at Sittingbourne and several Scottish gas works had narrow gauge steam railways, too. Army and navy stores depots often used narrow gauge railways.

One Parliamentary line was the Post Office (London) Railway, otherwise known latterly as Mail Rail, a 2ft gauge electric underground railway under the centre of London. Planning started in 1911 but the undertaking was deferred by the First World War and was not opened until 1927.

Most photographs of industrial sites date from the 1930s or post-war, when owners were prepared to allow or tolerate the interests of visiting enthusiasts. Some would write to seek permission to visit, some would just turn up. The last steam-worked industrial lines were closed in the 1960s.

RIGHT For many enthusiasts, this early-20th-century postcard epitomises the industrial narrow gauge railway, with lightweight track in remote countryside. Near Frome, Somerset, the 2ft 3in gauge Vallis Vale Tramway carried roadstone from limestone quarries to Hapsford mill for processing. Horse-worked when photographed, it probably dated from the 1890s and was re-gauged to 2 feet and extended to serve more quarries in the 1930s. *Woolstone Bros*

RIGHT

LEFT **LEFT** Glenfaba brickworks, near Peel, Isle of Man, operated the last plateway in Britain. In common with most other railways on the island, it was of 3-foot gauge.
J. W. Sparrowe

RIGHT The Nantlle Railway, 3ft 6in gauge, was another ancient railway that lasted until the modern era, finally closing in 1963. Unusually for a Welsh mineral railway, it was sanctioned by an Act of Parliament; opened in 1828, it never carried passengers officially. It was taken over by the railway contractor Thomas Savin and incorporated into the Carnarvonshire Railway. In 1867 the route between Caernarfon and Penygroes was converted to standard gauge as a part of the line to Afon Wen, and the formation between Caernarfon and Dinas is now occupied by the Welsh Highland Railway. The London & North Western Railway's branch from Penygroes to Tal y Sarn replaced more of the railway in 1872. When a group of enthusiasts rode on the remaining stub on 5 May 1957 the haulage contractor was working for British Railways.
Harold D. Bowtell

RIGHT In South Wales, the Saundersfoot Railway was 4-foot gauge, carrying coal from the Daucleddau coalfield to the coast. Opened in 1829, it was the first railway in Pembrokeshire. It was converted from horse to locomotive working in 1874, when the Manning, Wardle 0-4-0ST in the photograph was supplied. It had no cab because of height restrictions in a tunnel in Saundersfoot, which is now a footpath. The railway closed in 1939. *J. Tompkins*

ABOVE The abandoned Dinorwic quarries still dominate the landscape at Llanberis, although some slate was quarried from pits, like the one shown here on 26 June 1956. The gauge, shared with the Penrhyn quarries at nearby Bethesda, was 1ft 10¾in. Barely visible, the locomotives are Hunslet 0-4-0STs *George B* and *Holy War*, both now preserved. *H. C. Casserley*

BELOW At Gilfach Ddu Dinorwic slate was transhipped onto the 4-foot-gauge Padarn Railway to be transported to Port Dinorwic on the Menai Strait. The building in the centre of this photograph, taken on 27 June 1958, is now part of the Llanberis Lake Railway's terminal building. The building on the right, then the quarry workshops, is now the Welsh National Slate Museum. One of the transporter wagons is preserved at the Narrow Gauge Railway Museum at Tywyn. *H. C. Casserley*

ABOVE In 1962 Hunslet 0-4-0ST
Linda approaches Port Penrhyn,
near Bangor, running parallel to
the standard gauge branch line
from the Chester & Holyhead
Railway. The quarry railway was
closed a few weeks later and in
1963 the locomotive was hired
to the Festiniog Railway, where
it remains a popular addition to
the FR fleet, rebuilt as a 2-4-0STT.

RIGHT The Dorothea slate quarry
in the Nantlle valley had several
steam locomotives. Bagnall 0-4-0ST
Wendy was built in 1919 for the
Votty & Bowydd quarry in Blaenau
Ffestiniog and was sold to Dorothea
in 1930. Out of use during the 1940s,
it was purchased by the Hampshire
Narrow Gauge Railway Preservation
Society in 1961 and subsequently
restored to working order.
P. Eckersley

RIGHT Built in Caernarfon, de Winton four-coupled vertical-boilered locomotives were popular with North Wales quarries, the Penmaenmawr granite quarries being one of the biggest customers, having eight 3-foot-gauge examples between 1891 and 1895. Several have been preserved, although only two (*Chaloner* and *Pendyffryn*, both 2-foot-gauge ex-Penyrorsedd, Nantlle) are in working order at the time of publication. Photographed on the wharf at Penmaenmawr on 12 August 1953, *Watkin* is one of the locomotives now displayed at Penrhyn Castle, near Bangor.
H. C. Casserley

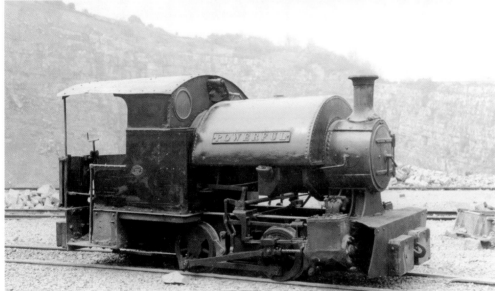

LEFT One of the lesser-known North Wales stone quarries was at Llandulas, on the North Wales coast between Abergele and Colwyn Bay, where limestone was both quarried and processed, and its railway had the unusual gauge of 2ft 10¼in. The Bagnall 0-4-0ST *Powerful* was built in 1911 and scrapped in 1958. Its buffer plank and cylinder cover reveal that it has been in trouble at some stage; its appearance has also been altered by modifying its cab and footplate to enable it to pass through a tunnel.

LEFT Granite was quarried at several quarries in Leicestershire, and Cliffe Hill, near Markfield, had a 2-foot-gauge railway to carry stone to the Midland Railway's Leicester-Coalville line. The railway was closed in 1948 and the locomotives were abandoned. Two of the seven Bagnall 0-4-0STs used were rescued and may be seen in working order: *Peter*, illustrated, is at the Amberley Museum in Sussex, and *Isabel* at the Amerton Railway in Staffordshire.
G. Alliez

Cable railways of various types were usually used to transport minerals from a quarry. This double-track 3-foot-gauge incline carried iron ore from Eastwell quarry in Leicestershire, the weight of the loaded wagons going down hauling the empties back up; the gradient was 1 in 4 at its steepest. At the foot of the incline, photographed on 15 July 1959, the ore was transferred to standard gauge wagons for onward shipment via the Great Northern & London & North Western Joint Railway between Melton Mowbray and Bottesford. *H. C. Casserley*

RIGHT Several other East Midlands iron ore quarries used narrow gauge railways, the Kettering system also using the 3-foot gauge. Little regard was paid to crew comfort when Black, Hawthorn 0-4-0ST No 2 entered service in 1879. Photographed on 14 April 1959, the locomotive was scrapped in 1963. Two others of the same type still exist but neither is in working order. *R. M. Casserley*

RIGHT Kay & Company's works at Southam, Warwickshire, was known for the fleet of six attractive Peckett 0-6-0STs obtained between 1903 and 1923 that worked the company's lime quarry. Having them named after geological ages made them even more attractive. The quarry tramway was closed in 1956 when the four surviving steam locomotives were laid aside. They were all purchased for preservation, *Liassic* being exported to Canada until it returned in 2012. *Mesozoic* spent some time in E. L. Pitt & Company's scrapyard at Brackley, Northamptonshire, where it was seen on 30 April 1966. *Jurassic* and *Triassic* have both been steamed on their original boilers but at the time of writing none of them are in working order.

ABOVE The railways of the Furzebrook clay mines of Pike Brothers, Fayle & Company, near Wareham, Dorset, used the unusual gauge of 2ft 8in. The company also had an unusual policy for naming its locomotives, using Latin numerals. Illustrated is the third addition to the fleet, 1886-built Manning, Wardle 0-6-0ST *Tertius*. It did not look like this when it left the maker's works, but in 1951 the boiler from the company's 3ft 9in-gauge 1868-built Lewin 0-4-0T *Tiny*, which had worked at the Norden clay mines near Corfe Castle until 1948, was fitted. Having a wider firebox that would not sit in the frames, the locomotive assumed a top-heavy appearance. Photographed on 20 January 1956, *Tertius* was scrapped in 1959.
R. M. Casserley

BELOW The Pentewan Railway in Cornwall was constructed to carry china clay from St Austell to the harbour at Pentewan. It was about 4-foot gauge when opened with horse haulage in 1829, and was rebuilt to 2ft 6in gauge for locomotives in 1874. Passenger carriage appears to have been limited to Sunday School excursions and the like, the passengers travelling in wagons. 2-6-2T *Pioneer* was built by the Yorkshire Engine Company for the Navy's Chattenden & Upnor Railway in 1903 and was obtained from the War Department in 1912. The railway was closed in 1918 when *Pioneer* and another locomotive were sold to the WD. Some track and former railway buildings are to be seen at Pentewan.

LEFT The German company Freudenstein only supplied one locomotive to the British market, this 0-4-0WT built circa 1901 and taken by Penlee & St Ives Quarries for use at Penlee, near Penzance. The most westerly industrial line in England, the quarry railway was constructed to carry stone to Newlyn harbour, half a mile away. The locomotive was withdrawn in 1946 and kept on the harbourside at Newlyn until 1994, when it was donated to the Leighton Buzzard Railway; it is now displayed at the LBR's Stonehenge works.

LEFT Despite a name associating it with carboniferous limestone hills in Somerset, this little Bagnall 0-4-0ST has nothing to do with stone or quarrying for it belonged to the Oakhill Brewery Company. A 2ft 6in-gauge railway 1½ miles long was completed in 1904 to carry brewery products and constituents between the brewery and the Somerset & Dorset Joint Railway at Binegar. *Mendip* was built in 1903 and sold in 1920, when the railway was closed; no doubt road transport had become more convenient.

RIGHT Located on the Thames near Erith, Callender's Cable & Construction Company Ltd's cable works had an extensive 3ft 6in-gauge railway that served two piers. Three oil-fired Bagnall 0-4-0STs were later joined by two diesel locomotives. Two of the former survived the railway's closure in 1968 to be converted to 2-foot gauge and coal-firing. *Sir Tom*, named after a company director, has recently been restored to work in the industrial environment to be found at the Threlkeld Quarry and Mining Museum in the Lake District.

ABOVE Bowater's Sittingbourne Railway was probably the largest non-military industrial narrow gauge railway system in England. Connecting Edward Lloyds Ltd's Sittingbourne paper mill with a dock on Milton Creek from 1908, the 2ft 6in-gauge railway was extended to the company's new dock at Ridham, on the banks of the Swale, a tributary of the Medway, in 1913, a length of 3½ miles. The railway also served a new mill built alongside it at Kemsley in 1924. The dock and the mills had several miles of sidings.

Steam locomotives were supplied by Bagnall (five), Kerr, Stuart (five) and Manning, Wardle (one), either as 0-4-2STs or 0-6-2Ts. Exceptionally,

one of the Bagnalls was an articulated 0-4-4-0T. Two further Bagnalls were fireless locomotives, a type rarely used on narrow gauge lines. Bagnall 0-6-2T *Triumph* is hauling a train of pulp to Sittingbourne on 11 August 1953. Passenger trains were also run for employees. The railway was the last steam-operated industrial narrow gauge railway when it was closed in 1969. A part of the railway between Sittingbourne and Kemsley is operated as a tourist attraction and most of the locomotives have been preserved, with two exceptions to be seen at Kemsley or on the Great Whipsnade Railway in Bedfordshire. *R. M. Casserley*

RIGHT At its peak the Royal Arsenal at Woolwich had 30 miles of 18-inch-gauge track and 120 miles of standard gauge covering 1,300 acres. The first narrow gauge locomotives were supplied in 1871, and by 1916 72 four-coupled locomotives had been supplied by eight different builders. Photographed on 25 May 1932, *Manchester* was one of the last batch, built by Avonside in Bristol; it was scrapped circa 1956. Another of this batch, *Woolwich*, is preserved at the Crossness pumping station in nearby Abbey Wood. The spark-arresting chimney indicates use in areas where explosives were handled. *H. C. Casserley*

LEFT The South Metropolitan Gas Company's Old Kent Road, Peckham, gas works accommodated what was possibly the closest narrow gauge steam railway to the centre of London. The 3-foot-gauge railway was used to transport coke around the site. *Concord* and *Unity* were 2-4-0T Bagnalls built in 1892 and 1898; they were sold for scrap in 1955. Although gas-making ended here in 1953, the site is still used to store gas.

RIGHT Bagnall 0-4-0STs were as popular with English industrial users as the Hunslet 0-4-0STs were with Welsh quarry owners. In this case, the circular fireboxes made them cheaper to build and to buy. The Birmingham Tame & Rea District Drainage Board used five at its Minworth sewage works; No 87001, seen here on 4 March 1961, was built in 1918. Steam working ended in 1961 and No 87001 passed to the City of Birmingham Museum of Science and Industry. Still owned by the museum, it is regularly steamed at the Abbey pumping station in Leicester where it is named *Leonard*. *P. Eckersley*

RIGHT High in the remote Lowther hills in Dumfriesshire, the Wanlockhead Mining Company mined lead sulphide, galena, which is widespread in the district. The 20-inch-gauge railway used steam locomotives from the early 1920s. *Wanlock*, a Barclay 0-4-0WT, was built in 1923 and is seen here on 30 July 1931; it was scrapped on site when the mines closed in 1938. At 1,531 feet above sea level, Wanlockhead is Britain's highest village. It was served by the Caledonian Railway's Leadhills & Wanlockhead Light Railway, a 7-mile branch that joined the West Coast Main Line at Elvanfoot, close to Beattock summit, from 1901. A part of the trackbed at Wanlockhead is used by the Leadhills & Wanlockhead Railway, a 2-foot-gauge enthusiast-led tourist development. *H. C. Casserley*

ABOVE The works of the London & North Western Railway and Lancashire & Yorkshire Railway at Crewe and Horwich both had 18-inch-gauge internal railways for moving materials about. *Wren* was the last of three locomotives built by Beyer, Peacock at Gorton for the opening of the LYR's Horwich works in 1887. Over the years the 18-inch-gauge railway was extended to about 7 miles, and five more similar locomotives had been built in-house by 1901. In the light of experience, the LYR-built examples were enhanced by the provision of a saddle tank, the Beyer, Peacock specimens being modified to match. Another afterthought was the adaptation of wagons to serve as tenders to carry coal, tools and coupling bars. The railway's use declined after the First World War, and by 1948 only *Wren* remained in use, accompanied by a Hudswell, Clarke four-wheeled diesel locomotive transferred from the Crewe system in the 1930s. Withdrawn in 1962, *Wren* became part of the National Collection and is now displayed at the National Railway Museum.

RIGHT One of the most unusual narrow gauge railways was to be found at the Guinness brewery in Dublin. To cope with a restricted site on two levels, brewery engineer Samuel Geoghegan devised a system using 1ft 10in-gauge locomotives built to make the most of a restricted loading gauge. The difference in levels was accommodated by a spiral, in tunnel, on a 1 in 39 gradient. The first locomotive was built by Avonside in 1882, then 18 more were built in Dublin by William Spence between 1887 and 1921. To deal with the short 5ft 3in-gauge run between the brewery and the Great Southern & Western Railway's Kingsbridge goods yard, Geoghegan put in hand a system whereby a narrow gauge locomotive could be hoisted into a 5ft 3in gauge haulage wagon and propel it at low speed by means of rollers and gears. Diesel locomotives started to replace steam from 1947 and took over completely by 1965. Parts of the railway had become redundant by 1964, and the last train ran in 1975.

Photographed on 20 June 1961, No 23 (built in 1921) is standing in front of the hoist while two other locos in haulage wagons are visible behind. Four locomotives have been preserved: No 13 (1895) at the Narrow Gauge Railway Museum, Tywyn, No 17 (1902) by Guinness, No 20 (1905) at the Ulster Folk & Transport Museum, Cultra, County Down, and No 23 (with a haulage wagon) at the Amberley Museum in West Sussex. *P. Eckersley*

ABOVE As the photograph shows, the Edinburgh & Leith Corporations' Gas Commissioners Granton gas works had both standard and 2-foot-gauge railways. On the narrow gauge there were four of these tiny Barclay 0-4-0Ts. Seen in action on 11 June 1960, No 9 was built in 1925. In 1968 it was sold for preservation, and in 1993 took up residence on the Groudle Glen Railway, Isle of Man, with the name *Jack*. Sold to an owner based in England in 1996, it is often seen visiting different railways. No 5 is also preserved and in 2013 was transferred to Beamish, 'The Living Museum of the North', in 2013. Glasgow Corporation's gas department had similar locomotives working on a 2ft 6in-gauge system at the Provan gas works; one is preserved in original condition at the Welshpool & Llanfair Light Railway, while another has been rebuilt as a 2-foot-gauge locomotive with a saddle tank and is based in the South of England. *H. C. Casserley*

BELOW The widening of the East Coast Main Line at Hadley Wood, south of Potter's Bar, in the 1950s was probably one of the last major surface contracts to use a narrow gauge railway.

ABOVE Based in Ross on Wye, Alan Keef Ltd is a well-established railway supply company that has earned a reputation for its work with narrow gauge railways, locomotives and rolling stock. On its 21 September 2013 annual open day the company displayed two metre-gauge Krauss 0-4-0Ts that it had restored for a German customer. *Author*

BELOW Opened in 1927, the Post Office (London) Railway was closed in 2003. 6½ miles long, it connected the main line stations at Paddington and Liverpool Street with six sorting offices and was electrified at 440v DC using a centre pick-up rail, the unmanned trains operating automatically. Seen in one of the dead-end tunnels at Mount Pleasant sorting office on 14 June 1995, unit No 32 had been built by Hunslet in 1982. At the date of the photograph it had received a cosmetic overhaul. The diversion of travelling post offices into the rail-connected mail distribution centre at Willesden in 1996 contributed to the decision to close the system. The British Postal Museum & Archive has announced its intention to re-open a part of the system as a tourist attraction in a new museum and archive development at Mount Pleasant. *Author*

Ireland and the Isle of Man

4

In the British Isles it was in Ireland and the Isle of Man that the use of the 3-foot gauge for what might be called secondary railways was taken to its ultimate, although in the latter's case its use for the island's main arterial communications made it anything but secondary. The Irish railways concerned are shown in the accompanying table.

Ireland was also covered by the aforementioned 1846 Gauge of Railways Act, wherein it was declared that its standard gauge should be 5ft 3in. The Act was not applicable to the Isle of Man, but in any event the 3-foot gauge became the de facto sub-standard gauge on both islands without further legislation. It happened that the first 3-foot-gauge public lines on both islands were opened within a short time of each other, in 1874 and 1875; that in Ireland had been a private mineral line, the Glenariff Railway, opened in 1872.

❧

Authority for the first narrow gauge railways in **Ireland** was obtained by legislation in the Westminster Parliament, the earliest legislated use of a sub-5ft 3in gauge being the Ballymena, Cushendall & Red Bay Railway's 1872 Act, which permitted a gauge of not less than 2 feet and not exceeding 3 feet. The 3-foot gauge was first specified by the Larne & Ballyclare Act in 1873. The West Donegal Railway's 1879 Act was the first to impose a speed restriction, of 25mph, incidentally.

It will be noticed that some of the railways displayed features associated with tramways, particularly roadside running or the enclosure of the locomotive motion. The Clogher Valley Railway was one such, its main line even running down the centre of Main Street in Fivemiletown.

The Tramways (Ireland) Act 1860 had authorised the construction of 5ft 3in-gauge tramways worked by animals, the latter restriction being removed by the Tramways (Ireland) Amendment Act in 1871 while also applying the Regulation of Railways Acts 1840-71 when

locomotives were used. A further Amendment Act in 1881 restricted speeds to 10mph generally and 6mph in towns and villages. In 1883 the Tramways & Public Companies Act lifted the maximum speed to 12mph outside towns and villages and removed it altogether where a tramway was more than 30 feet from the centre of any public road.

The 1883 Act also covered the use of Treasury-supported local authority guarantees to such an extent that several 'tramways' were promoted in the years following. Such guarantees were intended to encourage investment and open up remote areas. However, most railways ran out of cash before they were completed and none of them were profitable to any extent.

The final legislative influence on Irish narrow gauge railway development was the Light Railways (Ireland) Act, which received the Royal Assent in 1889. This made public funds available as free grants or loans, but only two narrow gauge schemes took advantage of it and they were both parts of existing railways.

One railway that is traditionally included in reviews of Irish narrow gauge lines is the Listowel & Ballybunion, opened in 1888, a Lartigue monorail that arguably had no gauge at all. Reference to it draws attention to the tales that became attached to some Irish railways: in the case of Listowel, the problem of the farmer sending a cow to market having to send two calves to balance it, which would then be balanced when returning to the farm.

Another well-known story is that of the encounter of the music hall singer Percy French with the West Clare Railway, which resulted in his song 'Are you right there Michael? Are you right?' Less well known, and of a different tenor, is the case of ex-head constable Irvine, appointed station master at Cork by the Cork & Muskerry Light Railway in 1887, which was raised in Parliament.

A notice had been posted calling for the railway to be boycotted unless Irvine was removed from his position. Citizens were unemployed and hungry while Irvine, who had a pension and owned

Irish railways

Railway	Opened	Closed	Length (miles)	Notes
Ballycastle Railway[1]	1880	1950	16¼	County Antrim. Taken over by the London Midland & Scottish Railway in 1925. Closed by the Ulster Transport Authority.
Ballymena & Larne Railway[1]	1878	1950	31	County Antrim. Taken over by the Belfast & Northern Counties Railway in 1903. Closed by the Ulster Transport Authority. Ruling gradient 1 in 36.
Ballymena, Cushendall & Red Bay Railway[1]	1875	1940	16¼	County Antrim. Taken over by the Belfast & Northern Counties Railway in 1884. Essatholan Summit, 1,045 feet, was the highest in Ireland.
Castlederg & Victoria Bridge Tramway[1]	1883	1933	7¼	County Tyrone.
Cavan & Leitrim Railway[2]	1887	1959	48½	
Clogher Valley Railway[2]	1887	1941	37	County Tyrone. In Northern Ireland from 1921, run by Tyrone and Fermanagh County Councils from 1928.
Cork & Muskerry Light Railway[2]	1887	1934	15½	County Cork. Operated the Donoughmore Light Railway (8½ miles) from St Anne's from 1893.
Cork, Blackrock & Passage Railway[1]	1850	1932	16	County Cork. 5ft 3in-gauge until 1900, when the Cork-Blackrock section became the only Irish narrow gauge line with a double track. Extensions from Passage West to Monkstown and Crosshaven opened in 1902 and 1904 respectively.
Donegal Railway[1]	1863	1959	124	County Donegal. Strabane-Stranorlar (13¾ miles) opened as the 5ft 3in-gauge Finn Valley Railway (FVR). 3-foot-gauge West Donegal Railway (WDR), Stranolar-Druminin (14 miles) opened 1882, Druminin-Donegal (4 miles) opened 1889, operated by the FVR. The Killybegs Light Railway (19 miles) and the Stranorlar & Glenties Light Railway (24 miles) were government-funded extensions opened in 1893 and 1895 respectively. In 1894 the Donegal Railway was created by merging the FVR and WDR. Strabane-Londonderry (14¼ miles) opened 1900; the FVR was re-gauged to 3 feet. Donegal-Ballyshannon (15½ miles) opened 1905. Transferred to Great Northern (Ireland) Railway and Midland Railway in 1906 and operated by the County Donegal Railways Joint Committee.
Letterkenny Railway[1]	1883	1953	15½	Operated by the Londonderry & Lough Swilly Railway from a junction at Cuttymanhill on the Farland Point branch.
Londonderry & Lough Swilly Railway[1]	1863	1953	99	Londonderry-Farland Point (9 miles) opened 1863, Tooban Junction-Buncrana (6 miles) opened in 1864, both 5ft 3in gauge. Re-gauged to 3 feet to suit the Letterkenny Railway in 1885. Government-sponsored, the extensions to Cardonagh (18 miles) and Burtonport (49¾ miles) opened in 1901 and 1903. Crossed into County Donegal. Cross-border operation from 1922. The railway company continued in existence as a road-service operator until 2014.
Schull & Skibbereen Railway[2]	1886	1947	15½	County Cork
South Clare Railway[2]	1887	1961	27	County Clare. Run by the West Clare Railway.
Strabane & Letterkenny Railway[1]	1909	1960	19¼	County Tyrone/County Donegal. Cross-border operation after 1921. Operated by the County Donegal Railways Joint Committee.
Tralee & Dingle Light Railway[2]	1891	1953	32	County Kerry.
West Clare Railway[2]	1892	1961		County Clare

[1] Authorised by Act(s) of Parliament

[2] Authorised by the Tramways Act 1860 following the Tramways & Public Companies (Ireland) Act 1883

ABOVE Ballycastle station is seen here in 1938. Opened in 1880, the Ballycastle Railway was 16¼ miles long, connecting Ballycastle with the Belfast & Northern Counties Railway at Ballymoney, both in County Antrim. Impoverished before it was opened, its main source of traffic was the terminus. It was taken over by the London Midland & Scottish Railway (Northern Counties Committee) in 1924; the Committee had been a subsidiary of the Midland Railway, which had taken over the BNCR in 1903. This allowed economies to be made and newer rolling stock to be introduced. The line was closed by the Ulster Transport Authority in 1950. The locomotive is one of several 2-6-2Ts initially built by Beyer, Peacock, then by the NCC at its York Road works in Belfast. The carriages are those built at York Road in 1928 for the Ballymena & Larne Railway's boat train services, transferred to Ballycastle in 1933. At 50 feet, they were the longest to operate on Irish narrow gauge railways and the only ones to have corridor connections.

property, was drawing a salary from a company established to benefit the local populace. Not only that, he 'was known as the most insulting bigot in the force.' Since the notice was erected Irvine was 'jeered at and otherwise interfered with at his place of employment.' He resigned, saying that the hours of duty had been much greater than he had expected when accepting the appointment.

It is clear that the railways were lightly managed and adapted their working practices to suit local needs. Generally, traffic was mostly agricultural in nature although iron ore was carried in Antrim, and coal from Arigna kept the Cavan & Leitrim Railway going for a long time. The last traffic on the Tralee & Dingle Railway was the weekly market cattle trains.

The creation of the Irish Free State in 1922 affected the railways in various ways that will not be explored here, except that in 1924 the Great Southern Railways Company was established to own all the railways in the south. In 1945 the GSR was dissolved and its assets, together with those of the Dublin United Transport Company, were transferred to Córas Iompair Éireann.

Attempts to reduce costs included the successful introduction of railcars on the County Donegal Railways from 1930. Railcars were also used on the Clogher Valley and West Clare lines. The latter was the only narrow gauge railway modernised by Córas Iompair Éireann, which equipped it with new railcars and diesel locomotives less than ten years before the line was closed.

Since the lines were closed various preservation attempts have met with mixed fortunes. In 1970, for example, Lord O'Neill built a 3-foot-gauge tourist railway in the grounds of Shane's Castle, County Antrim, using steam locomotives acquired from Bord na Móna, the Irish Peat Board, and the British Aluminium Company at Larne, but it closed in 1994. A 1½-mile section of the Tralee & Dingle Railway was reopened using an original locomotive repatriated from the USA in 1993, but ceased operating in 2006, when the locomotive required a new boiler.

Several attempts have been made to revive sections of the County

Donegal Railway, the Fintown Railway (An Mhuc Dhubh), being the most successful, with the reconstruction of 3 miles of track alongside Lough Finn and the use of one of the original railcars.

In Dromod station yard, the Cavan & Leitrim Railway is the focus of a wide-ranging museum collection, with a short demonstration line in operation since 1995. For motive power it has a steam locomotive built around the frames of a Kerr, Stuart 0-4-2 and Avonside 0-6-0T *Nancy*, which spent its working life in Leicestershire iron ore quarries.

Irish industry also made use of the 3ft gauge, primarily Bord Na Móna, the Irish Peat Board, which still has hundreds of miles of railways extending across the bogs of central Ireland. Established in 1946 to take over the responsibilities of the Turf Development Board, established in 1933, the Bord's railways are used in the harvesting of peat for use as fuel. Some 200 miles of temporary track are laid to follow the cutting edge during each harvesting season. Three steam locomotives acquired in 1949 were sold in 1969 and the Bord now builds its own diesel-hydraulic locomotives.

TOP RIGHT The Ballymena & Larne Railway was 13½ miles long and fully opened in 1878. The 4¼ mile-long branch from Ballyboley to Ballyclare was extended another 2 miles to Doagh in 1884. The BNCR look over in 1889. A strike brought about the withdrawal of the passenger service in 1933, and the line between Ballyboley and Ballymena was closed in 1940; the remainder was closed in 1950. 2-4-2T No 103 was photographed at Ballymena. Built at York Road in 1919, it was withdrawn in 1938. The LMSR crest is mounted on the cabside.

CENTRE RIGHT In the north Midlands of Ireland, the Cavan & Leitrim Railway between Dromod and Belturbet, 33¾ miles, was opened in 1887. The 14¾-mile branch line from Ballinamore to Arigna was opened in 1888, and was classified as a tramway; it accounted for four of the eight 4-4-0Ts obtained from Robert Stephenson being fitted with condensing gear and having their lower parts enclosed in the style of tram engines; from 1898 either type of locomotive was allowed to work the branch.

Unusually, the promoters had not only underestimated the line's operating costs, but had also underestimated the available traffic; resolving the latter did nothing to resolve the former. The shortage of funds meant that the extension to coal mines 4 miles from Arigna had to wait until the government took control in 1917, but was not completed until 1920; in 1930 the last 2¼ miles of the extension was closed, although the mine continued to provide traffic until the railway closed in 1959.

Shown much altered, No 7 *Olive* was one of the locomotives supplied to work on the Arigna tramway. It lost its name circa 1925 and after several years out of use was withdrawn in 1945. One of the Cavan & Leitrim's 12 tramway-style carriages is stabled behind the locomotive.

BOTTOM RIGHT An early-20th-century scene at Drumshambo, on the Arigna branch. *Tarleton Publishing Company, Dublin*

RAILWAY STATION, DRUMSHAMBO.

TOP LEFT In 1934 the Great Southern Railways sent the Cavan & Leitrim four Cork, Blackrock & Passage Railway Neilson 2-4-2Ts that had been overhauled after that railway had been closed in 1932. Four locomotives were also transferred from the Tralee & Dingle Railway between 1941 and 1957. On 6 August 1957, shortly after it had arrived, one of the latter, No 6T, a Hunslet 2-6-0T, was photographed climbing to the Arigna mine with empty wagons. *Alan Donaldson*

CENTRE LEFT One of the six Clogher Valley Railway's Sharp, Stewart 0-4-2Ts stands in the carriage shed at Fivemiletown. The main line westwards to Maguiresbridge is to the right of the shed. Opened in 1887, the CVR struggled financially more than most and was closed in 1941. It was 37 miles long, running more or less east-west between Maguiresbridge and Tynan, mostly on the roadside and connecting with the Great Northern Railway at each end. A trial with a County Donegal Railway railcar in 1932 was followed by the acquisition of a similar unit in 1933; sold to the CDR after the line closed, the railcar is preserved at the Ulster Folk & Transport Museum. In 1934 the CVR also acquired a Castlederg & Victoria Bridge Tramway Hudswell, Clarke 2-6-2T tram engine.

BOTTOM LEFT Serving the hinterland to the west of Cork, the Cork & Muskerry Light Railway's best-known station was Blarney, serving the castle with the famous stone of the same name, 8½ miles from Cork. There was also a 9-mile branch to Coachford. The Donoughmore Extension Light Railway was an 8½-mile branch from St Anne's on the Blarney branch; nominally independent, it was operated by the CMLR.

Cork & Muskerry Light Railway No 1 was one of three 2-4-0Ts built by Falcon for the railway's opening in 1887. The trio were rebuilt as 4-4-0Ts in 1890-94, Brush supplying two more 4-4-0Ts in 1898 and 1904. In the meantime Kitson had supplied an 0-4-2WT in 1888 and Thomas Green two 0-4-4Ts in 1892 and 1893. The only gestures towards the line's tramway status are the cowcatcher and the bell, mounted on the tank top.

RIGHT The tramway nature of the CMLR is illustrated by this fine view of a train at Carrigrohane, 3½ miles from Cork. No 7 was the first of the two Brush-built 4-4-0Ts. The system was closed in 1934. Close to the CMLR's Cork terminus was the western terminus of the 6½-mile Cork, Blackrock & Passage Railway, which opened in 1850 to the 5ft 3in gauge, was converted to 3-foot gauge in 1900, and extended in stages to Crosshaven, 9½ miles, by 1904. It was closed in 1932.

ABOVE The 3-foot-gauge railway network centred on Strabane in Donegal was taken over by the Irish Great Northern Railway and the Derby-based Midland Railway in 1906 and subsequently managed by their County Donegal Railways Joint Committee. From Strabane there were branches to Londonderry (14½ miles), Donegal (31¾ miles) and Letterkenny (19¼ miles); from Donegal there were branches to Killybegs (19 miles) and Ballyshannon (15½ miles); and from Stranorlar there was a branch to Glenties (24 miles), 124 miles in total.

The oldest section was opened as the 5ft 3in-gauge Finn Valley Railway, from Stranorlar to Strabane, in 1863. The 3-foot-gauge West Donegal Railway was opened to Druminin in 1882 and to Donegal in 1889. These companies merged as the Donegal Railway in 1892, the Finn Valley section being re-gauged to 3 feet in 1894; the Killybegs line had been opened in 1893. The Glenties branch was opened in 1895, the Londonderry line in 1900 and the Ballyshannon branch in 1905. Following the takeover, the connection to the Londonderry & Lough Swilly Railway at Letterkenny was opened in 1909. Timetabled services were withdrawn from the Glenties branch in 1947 and it was closed in 1952. Services to Londonderry ceased in 1954, the line being closed in 1955. The entire system was closed in 1959.

Sharp, Stewart 2-4-0T No 1 *Alice* was one of three built in 1881 and remained in service until 1926. By 1912 23 steam locomotives had been supplied for the system, the first withdrawals taking place as the last were being delivered.

TOP RIGHT In contrast to No 1, No 15 *Mourne* was a 4-6-4T, one of four supplied in 1904 by Nasmyth, Wilson. It was withdrawn in 1952.

CENTRE RIGHT The first locomotives obtained by the Joint Committee were three Nasmyth, Wilson 2-6-4Ts delivered in 1907. No 16 *Donegal* is seen shunting on 23 June 1937, when at least one van still retained its Donegal Railway branding. Later in that year No 16 became No 4 *Meenglas*, and is now preserved at the Foyle Valley Railway in Londonderry. *H. C. Casserley*

BELOW Supplied by Nasmyth, Wilson in 1912, 2-6-4T No 2 *Blanche* was one of the last locomotives to enter service on the County Donegal system, taking the number of its 1881 predecessor withdrawn at the same time. Originally named *Strabane*, it received its new name in 1928. It is preserved at the Ulster Folk & Transport Museum.
H. C. Casserley

RIGHT The Donegal Railway was a pioneer in the use of internal combustion to reduce operating expenses. Its first railcar was a four-wheeled 10hp petrol-engined vehicle with accommodation for ten passengers, introduced in 1906. Rebuilt in 1920, it is now exhibited at the Ulster Folk & Transport Museum. Railcar No 2, illustrated here, was acquired from the Derwent Valley Light Railway and was rebuilt and re-gauged at the Great Northern Railway's Dundalk works before entering service in 1926. Powered by a 22hp petrol engine, it had room for 17 passengers, and luggage space was provided on the roof. It was withdrawn in 1934.

LEFT Later railcars were quite sophisticated for the period, with a mechanical traction unit articulated from the passenger compartment. Nos 16-20, built between 1936 and 1951, had 102hp Gardner diesel engines and seating for 41-43 passengers. They could also tow one or two vans. No 17, seen here, was written off after a collision in 1949.

LEFT *Phoenix*, which entered service in 1933, was a diesel locomotive, despite being No 11 in the County Donegal railcar list. It had been supplied as an experimental steam tractor to the Clogher Valley Railway in 1928 but had probably been underpowered in that form. It has outlived both railways and is to be seen at the Ulster Folk & Transport Museum. *P. B. Whitehouse*

ABOVE The highly unusual Listowel & Ballybunion Railway was located in Kerry, connecting the small coastal resort of Ballybunion with the Waterford & Limerick Railway, 9¼ miles distant. Opened in 1888, it was built according to the patents of Charles Lartigue, a monorail carried on 'A' frames with motive power and rolling stock balanced astride them. Lartigue had wished to develop a rail system that could be laid easily without levelling the ground, and is said to have been inspired by the loading of camels while he was working in a north African desert. Three double locomotives were built by Hunslet and a number of carriages and wagons by Falcon. Despite the simplicity of its track, the railway was unnecessarily complicated in its equipment and operation. Revenue from tourists carried in the summer was insufficient to cover expenses during the winter and the railway company entered receivership in 1897; it was closed 1924. One of the locomotives and its crew pose for the photographer at Listowel depot. A boiler from one of the other locomotives is on the right.

BELOW No 3 is turned on the turntable at Ballybunion while the passenger stock stands in the station. Referred to as 'the Lartigue', the railway is still held in fond regard in the locality and in 1995 a short demonstration line was established with a diesel engine locomotive.

ABOVE With branches to Cardonagh and Burtonport, the Londonderry & Lough Swilly Railway's 98¾ miles in the wilds of Donegal came closest to matching its County Donegal neighbour for route mileage than any other Irish narrow gauge line. Like the Finn Valley section of the Donegal Railway, the LLSR also had a section re-gauged from 5ft 3in. From Londonderry, the railway originally comprised branches to Farland Point and Buncrana, diverging at Tooban Junction and opened in 1863 and 1864 respectively. The Farland Point branch was abandoned in 1866 but reinstated on a modified alignment when the independent 3-foot-gauge Letterkenny Railway was opened from Tooban Junction to Letterkenny in 1883. Operating the LR and converting the Buncrana line to 3-foot gauge in 1885 created a system of 37 miles. Extensions of the Buncrana line to Cardonagh (18½

miles) in 1901 and the Letterkenny line to Burtonport (49¾ miles) in 1903 were government schemes, the latter under the name of the Letterkenny & Burtonport Extension Railway.

This works photograph is of one of two 4-6-2Ts delivered by Hudswell, Clarke in Leeds in 1899. At the time they were the largest locomotives on the railway; two more were built in 1901.

BELOW Seen on 19 April 1948 at the LLSR's Graving Dock terminus in Londonderry – the only narrow gauge railway station to have an overall roof, albeit only covering part of the platform – No 10 was one of two Kerr, Stuart 4-6-2Ts delivered in 1904. The spacing between the tracks is indicative of this part of the railway having once been 5ft 3in gauge. *H. C. Casserley*

RIGHT Barclay 4-6-0T No 3 was one of a batch of four delivered to work the Burtonport extension in 1902. When new it was lined out and lettered L&BER. It remained in service until the railway's closure in 1954.

BELOW The Burtonport 4-6-0Ts proved to be underpowered, resulting in the acquisition of the only tender locomotives to work on the Irish narrow gauge. Two 4-8-0s were supplied by Hudswell, Clarke in 1905, and one of them is seen here on 17 September 1948. *Ian L. Wright*

LEFT The last new locomotives delivered to the Lough Swilly were a pair of chunky 4-8-4Ts built for the Burtonport extension in 1912. In terms of capability they outmatched the 0-6-0s by 350lb tractive effort.

Instead of finding ways to reduce operating expenses, from the 1930s the LLSR turned to road transport, operating bus services that were more convenient for its passengers. The Cardonagh extension was closed in 1935 and the Burtonport extension in 1940, the latter reopening as far as Gweedore (54 miles) in 1941. The latter was closed finally in 1947, the remainder of the railway in 1953.

ABOVE The Schull & Skibbereen Railway was another roadside line, 14¼ miles long, in County Cork. It ran along the south coast, connecting the Skibbereen terminus of the Cork, Bandon & South Coast Railway with Schull, a small coastal town. Opened in 1886, a half-mile extension to Schull pier was opened in 1893. The line struggled more than most – it was poorly made – and on 6 April 1887 services were suspended because none of the three Dick, Kerr 0-4-0 tram engines was fit to run. Money was borrowed to make good the deficiencies in the formation and permanent way and to purchase a new locomotive, a 4-4-0T of more traditional appearance,

which arrived from Nasmyth, Wilson in time for services to be resumed on 2 January 1888. In 1892 the railway was taken over by the local authorities guaranteeing the capital. The 4-4-0T was reboilered in 1908 and was photographed in this form running round at Skibbereen circa 1930.

BELOW Peckett 4-4-0Ts obtained in 1906 and 1914 replaced two of the tram engines. The second of these, No 3 *Kent*, is seen leaving Skibbereen, the layout being such that trains were reversed out of and into the station, which forms the backdrop to the photograph. *A. P. Hughes*

ABOVE The largest structure on the SSR was this 12-arch viaduct at Ballydehob, 9½ miles from Skibbereen; Ballydehob station is on the far side. The river is the Bawnaknockane, a tidal inlet.

In common with the other railways in the south, the Schull & Skibbereen was merged into the Great Southern Railways in 1925. Fuel shortages disrupted services during the war and the local bus service was extended to Schull in 1945. Another fuel shortage was responsible for services being cancelled after 25 January 1947 and the trains never ran again, the line being formally abandoned in 1956. *A. P. Hughes*

BELOW The Tralee & Dingle Railway was a 37¾-mile system serving the Dingle peninsula on the Irish west coast, making an interchange with the Waterford, Limerick & Western Railway at Tralee. Opened later than

intended, in 1891, it had a main line from Tralee to Dingle (31¾ miles) and a branch to Castlegregory (6 miles). Construction quality was poor and changes to the route were soon made, including a new viaduct at Curraduff, replacing the original structure after a train ran away there in 1893. The local authorities took control in 1896.

Hunslet supplied three 2-6-0Ts in 1889 and an 0-4-2T in 1892, the latter for the Castlegregory branch. The 2-6-0Ts were delivered with skirts protecting their motion, which were soon removed, while the 0-4-2T was a tram engine, capable of being driven from either end. No 5, photographed at Tralee soon after delivery in 1892, was another Hunslet 2-6-2T. Hunslet supplied 2-6-0Ts in 1898 and 1910, while Kerr, Stuart delivered 2-6-0Ts in 1902 and 1903. The Castlegregory loco was out of use by 1902 and one of the Kerr, Stuarts was withdrawn in 1928; the remainder continued in use until the 1950s. *T. J. Goodlake*

ABOVE The Tralee & Dingle passengers service was ended in 1939, the Castlegregory branch closing at the same time. From 1944 the goods service ran as required, but in 1947 operations were reduced to a service of cattle trains run in conjunction with the monthly fair at Dingle, which attracted the attention of some English enthusiasts before it was ended with the railway's closure in 1953. One of the cattle trains was photographed at Castlegregory Junction. *C. H. S. Owen*

BELOW Between 1939 and 1950 three locomotives were transferred away, two to the Cavan & Leitrim Railway and one to the West Clare Railway. In 1959 Hunslet 2-6-2T No 5 and the Cavan & Leitrim 4-4-0T *Lady Edith* were sold to Edgar Mead in the USA. No 5 was returned to Tralee in 1986 and was restored to work on a short section of the Tralee & Dingle Railway based at Blennerville, where this photograph was taken on 15 May 1992, the occasion of its first steaming. *D. M. Warren*

ABOVE Opened in 1892, the West Clare Railway operated its own railway between Ennis, on the Irish west coast and the terminus of the Midland Great Western Railway, and Kilkee, a distance of 48 miles, and the South Clare Railway, from Moyasta Junction to Cappa Pier (5 miles). Unusually, the junction had a triangular layout. The WCR had four Bagnall 0-6-0Ts while the SCR had three Dübs 0-6-2Ts. Thomas Green supplied three 2-6-2Ts between 1898 and 1901, No 2 *Ennis* being built in 1900. From 1902 Kerr, Stuart, Bagnall and Hunslet supplied 4-6-0Ts to the line.

BELOW Tralee & Dingle Railway No 5 was sent to the West Clare in 1953, staying there for only two years. It was photographed at Lahinch, 20 miles from Ennis, on a special working.

ABOVE In 1952 the West Clare Railway was modernised with the provision of four new railcars numbered in the Córas Iompair Éireann sequence. The new railcar trailers were constructed on the underframes of Tralee & Dingle Railway carriages at the same time. Three diesel locomotives were added to the railway's stock list in 1955 but, despite some local opposition, the railway was closed after the last trains on 31 January 1961.

BELOW After the railway was closed, South Clare 0-6-2T No 5 Slieve Callan was sent to Inchicore works, Dublin, for scrapping with the other stock, but somehow escaped. Wiser counsels prevailed when it was discovered there sometime later, and it was put on display at Ennis. In 2009 it was restored to working order by Alan Keef Ltd in England and operates on a short length of railway at Moyasta.

Independent and self-governing, the **Isle of Man** is a British Crown dependency set in the Irish Sea. It was a haven of 3 foot-gauge railways and remains the sole outpost of the genre, still with its original steam locomotives and Victorian carriages. The routes developed were very much constrained by the island's geography and geology.

The Isle of Man Railway Company, registered in 1872, built two railways, Douglas to Peel (opened in 1873) and Douglas to Port Erin (opened in 1874). Known as the South line, the latter is 15 miles long and features a climb of some 2 miles at 1 in 70 out of Douglas. Once outside the island's capital the line ran through open countryside, serving some larger communities as it got closer to Port Erin.

Crossing the island from east to west, the Peel line was shorter at just over 11 miles long. It also climbed out of Douglas, the 7 miles to the summit at Ballacurrey offering somewhat easier gradients to the enginemen. The line's biggest sources of traffic were its termini.

Beyer, Peacock supplied three 2-4-0Ts that were modified versions of 3ft 6in-gauge locomotives supplied to Norwegian State Railways. The basic design became the railway's standard, 14 locomotives having been supplied with minor modifications by 1926. Four-wheeled carriages obtained in 1873/74 were joined by bogie stock from 1881. From 1887 pairs of the four-wheeled stock were permanently coupled together, and from 1909 the bodies of the four-wheeled carriages were mounted in pairs on new bogie underframes.

The Manx Northern Railway's line to Ramsey was opened in 1879, making a junction with the IMR at St John's and providing a circuitous route across sparsely occupied countryside to connect Ramsey with the island's capital. In parts the line was routed along the clifftops, in sight of the sea. Glen Mooar and Glen Wyllin were crossed by three-span viaducts. The ruling gradient southwards was 1 in 100 at most.

Serving Foxdale, a small mining community 2½ miles from St John's, the Foxdale Railway was opened in 1886. Nominally independent of the MNR, the two companies shared directors and it was leased by the latter before it was opened. The branch climbed at 1 in 49 from St John's.

When opened, the MNR had two Sharp, Stewart 2-4-0Ts slightly larger than the IMR's Beyer, Peacocks and not dissimilar to the

Southwold locomotives supplied at the same time. Beyer, Peacock was able to offer a better price for a third locomotive required in 1880 because it also had an order for a single locomotive from the larger Manx company. In 1885 Dübs of Glasgow supplied an 0-6-0T for working the Foxdale branch. Carriages with Cleminson underframes were supplied by the Swansea Wagon Company.

The expiry of the Isle of Man Government's 25-year guarantee to pay 4% on £25,000 MNR preference shares in 1904 brought about its absorption into the IMR in 1905. The MNR's rolling stock was incorporated into IMR fleet lists, but the six-wheeled carriages were soon put into store at St John's; they had never been allowed onto IMR metals previously, anyway. The IMR's engineers did not think much of the Sharp, Stewarts, either, putting them on restricted duties; they were condemned in 1912.

As an undertaking, the IMR was quite successful, paying regular dividends to its shareholders, but by the 1950s paying the dividend became more important to the directors than maintaining the undertaking, which increasingly looked its age; the newest locomotive had been bought in 1926, the newest carriage three years earlier. The situation was aggravated as residents bought motor cars and tourists deserted the island in favour of cheap package holidays overseas.

The period from 1961 to 1978 was one of uncertainty for the IMR. The withdrawal of winter passenger services to Ramsey from 1961 and the purchase of two County Donegal Railway railcars, also in 1961, had little positive effect on the IMR's finances, and in November 1965 the entire system was closed without notice, allegedly for maintenance. From 1967 it was leased by Lord Ailsa and reopened in full. He introduced innovations, container trains, and a halt near Ronaldsway

BELOW The Isle of Man Railway's Beyer, Peacock 2-4-0T No 2 *Derby* was one of three locomotives available when the railway opened between Douglas and Peel in 1873. Seen here at Castletown, the locomotive was withdrawn in 1949 and scrapped in 1951, some parts being used on other locos. The four-wheeled brake van, E5, was built in 1876 and was used as a mobile store at Douglas between 1958 and 1963.

Airport, and ordered two locomotive boilers. The Ramsey line was not operated in 1968 and in September the remaining services were suspended. A grant enabled the south line to be reopened in 1969.

When Ailsa withdrew in 1972 the company resumed operating the railway. The south line was reopened later in the year, the remainder was lifted for scrap from 1974, and the now surplus land was sold to the government in 1975/76. The restriction of services to Port Erin-Castletown (5 miles) in 1975 did nothing for receipts.

As might be expected, very few visitors, the author among them, took the trouble to seek out the restricted railway service. Despite the operating loss, land and property sales enabled the shareholders to receive a 20% dividend.

Services were extended to Ballasalla in 1976, and at the end of the year the government agreed to subsidise services operating from Douglas in 1977. In January 1978 the company was nationalised, the government paying £250,000 for the remainder of the undertaking. With receipts from property sales set against capitalisation of £365,000, it looks as though the shareholders would have had most of their money back – something that few railway investors achieved.

Operations were placed under the control of the Manx Electric Railway Board, operator of the previously nationalised Manx Electric

ABOVE Traditionally, Douglas station was known for its terminal buildings, its platform canopies, the coal heap and the worn-out axle sets. The appearance of the coal heap is deceptive, for other photographs show that the large lumps conceal a great deal of smaller pieces and dust. The canopies were demolished in the 1970s.

Railway and Snaefell Mountain Railway. Later, the railways became part of the Department of Tourism and Leisure, now the Department of Community, Culture and Leisure. The railways, and buses, are managed by the Director of Public Transport.

Many changes have been made since the government took over. Despite the establishment of a museum at Port Erin in 1975, the years to 1987 saw the destruction of many original features and the sale of locomotives and stock. The routing of a sewer along the railway trackbed early in the 21st century provided the funds to renew the permanent way over most of the line, and several level crossings have been modernised. The value of the railway's heritage is now more appreciated and features, including traditional signalling at Douglas, are being restored. It is *the* place to experience early-20th-century 3-foot-gauge rail travel.

LEFT No 5 *Mona* was one of two locomotives supplied by Beyer, Peacock for the opening of the Port Erin line in 1874. They had larger water tanks and were more powerful than Nos 1-3. No 5 was rebuilt with a larger boiler in 1914. On 27 August 1957 the driver oils round while the fireman tells the foreman about a fishing trip on his last day off!

RIGHT Dübs 0-6-0T *Caledonia* is the only Manx Northern Railway locomotive still in working order. No 4 in the MNR fleet, it was obtained in 1885 to work Foxdale branch ore traffic. In 1895 it was hired out to haul construction trains on the Snaefell Mountain Railway, then became No 15 in the IMR fleet. Little used in the last years before nationalisation, it was the best locomotive available for snow clearing.

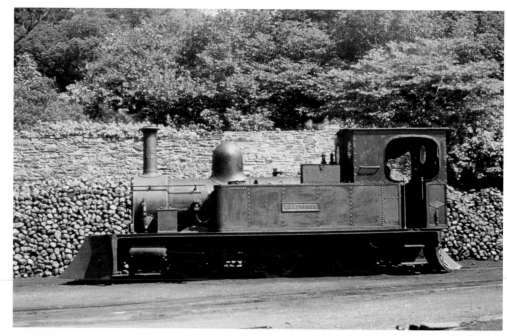

RIGHT Built in 1926, No 16 *Mannin* was the last of the Manx Beyer, Peacock 2-4-0Ts, an enlarged and modernised version of its predecessors. It was withdrawn at the end of the 1964 season, pretty much in the same condition as when it had left its maker's works. Since 1975 it has been an exhibit in the Port Erin museum, and is seen here at Douglas on 23 July 1997, whence it had been taken while the museum was refurbished.

ABOVE The goods yard at Douglas was rarely photographed. Seen on 10 June 1970, the assortment of wagons and service stock partially conceals a line of out-of-service locomotives. The van was built in 1984 and used in the breakdown train from 1925. The site is now a car park.

BELOW This fine Douglas departure scene is framed by the works and locomotive shed on the left and the carriage shed on the right. The stone buildings date from 1891. After many years in a dilapidated condition the carriage shed was demolished in favour of the transport department's headquarters and bus depot. New carriage sheds have been provided at both Douglas and Port Erin. In 1999 the 1892 signal box was relocated to the left of its original site.

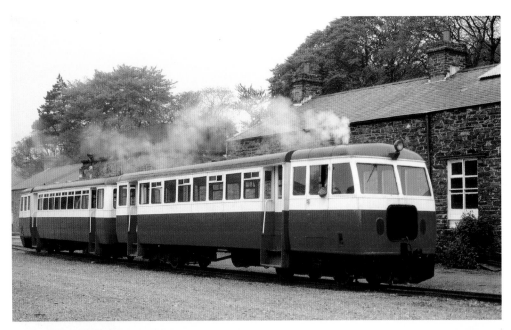

LEFT The County Donegal Railway's railcars were delivered in May 1961. Barely 10 years old, their power units had been built by Walker Brothers of Wigan, and their passenger saloons at the Great Northern Railway (Ireland)'s Dundalk works. After several years in traffic they were used as permanent way personnel carriers. A restoration project that was started in the 1990s remains incomplete. They were photographed being demonstrated at Douglas in May 1983. *Author*

LEFT The climb up to Port Soderick varies from 1 in 70 to 1 in 65, providing passengers with the sound of the locomotive working hard and views across the Irish Sea towards England. *Caledonia* was photographed on 26 July 1997. *Author*

RIGHT Palms at Santon provide a Mediterranean backdrop to trains passing on a fine day. 2-4-0T No 11 *Maitland* was photographed on 24 July 1996. *Author*

ABOVE New in 1908, 2-4-0T No 12 *Hutchinson* is seen arriving at Castletown on 28 July 1994. In 1979/80 No 12 was rebuilt with a new boiler, new tanks and a *Mannin*-style cab; the latter was replaced by a traditional-style cab in 2001. *Author*

BELOW The railcars are seen at Castletown on 30 May 1965, a luggage van coupled between them. *Michael Farr*

ABOVE Ballagawne crossing, on a minor road near Port St Mary, was one of several that were still permanently manned until recently. Automatic barriers were installed in 2002 and the building is currently unoccupied. 2-4-0T No 11 *Maitland*, built in 1905, was photographed on 20 July 1997. *Author*

BELOW 2-4-0T No 12 *Hutchinson* arrives at Port St Mary with the 11.50 from Port Erin on 16 June 1965. In 1926 Brake Composite F49, behind the engine, was the last carriage to be purchased by the Isle of Man Railway Company. It was also the first to be equipped with vacuum brakes, an innovation shared with No 16 *Mannin*, obtained at the same time. The Isle of Man Railway took a relaxed attitude to the use of continuous brakes despite a fatal accident when a train ran away and hit the buffers at Douglas in 1925. One of the problems was that the older locomotives with smaller boilers could not supply enough steam to create a vacuum. Use of the brake did not become mandatory until after nationalisation.

ABOVE Port Erin is essentially a large fishing village 12 miles from Douglas. Its railway, opened in 1874, was always the busiest on the Isle of Man. This busy scene at the station predates the Ailsa lease in 1967. A lorry is parked on the platform to collect and deliver parcels and spare carriages are stabled in the sidings to cope with peak demand. No 12 *Hutchinson* is coupled up in preparation to return to Douglas.

RIGHT Built for the opening of the Peel line in 1873, 2-4-0T No 1 *Sutherland* remained in service until 1964 and became an exhibit in the Port Erin museum from 1975. To mark the 125th anniversary of Manx steam in 1998 it was removed from the museum and returned to steam using the new boiler obtained for No 8 *Fenella*. The photograph was taken at Port Erin on 7 July 1998. *Author*

RIGHT The Isle of Man railways were known for the continued use of archaic signals long after such had been replaced elsewhere. Two different starting signals were photographed at St John's on 28 May 1968. Sadly, the array of archaic four-wheeled carriages that had been removed from the carriage shed to make way for disused locomotives was of no interest to the photographer. *Michael Farr*

ABOVE Peel is the only substantial settlement on the Manx west coast. Its railway, connecting it with Douglas, 11½ miles away, was opened in 1873, the first public railway on the Isle of Man. 2-4-0T No 5 *Mona* was captured on film taking water at Peel on 22 June 1965. The locomotive shed, on the right, was demolished in 1975, while the water tower has been developed as a visitor centre by the local heritage trust.

BELOW In common with the other IMR termini, Peel station was not without distinction, in this case built in 1911 to replace an earlier timber building. It was incorporated into the House of Mannanan museum in the 1990s. *Michael Farr*

RIGHT Ramsey station was better equipped for dealing with goods than passengers, with facilities for handling cattle, coal and minerals as well as a siding that ran through to the harbour. The locomotive shed is beyond the carriage shed. One of the railway's saloon carriages is at the front of the train stabled in the platform.

RIGHT At Ramsey on 21 June 1965, 2-4-0T No 8 *Fenella* waits to leave with the 4.05pm train for Douglas. The older locomotives were usually to be found on the lightly loaded Ramsey services.

BELOW This contemporary scene at Douglas shows locomotives in a traditional corporate livery and the bus depot on the site of the carriage shed.

5

Tourist railways

Without question, the first narrow gauge steam railway built solely to carry tourists was the **Snowdon Mountain Railway**, a rack railway of 800mm gauge that uses the Abt system. Built on private land without legal powers, its development followed the renaming of the North Wales Narrow Gauge Railways' Rhyd Ddu terminus as Snowdon in 1893 and the resulting diversion of tourists from Llanberis.

There are those, incidentally, who claim that Magnus **Volk's electric railway** in Brighton was the first narrow gauge tourist railway, rather than being a demonstrator of the principles of electric traction that happened to be at the seaside. Opened in 1883, its 2-foot gauge was widened to 2ft 9in the following year, and reduced to 2ft 8½in in 1886. Since 1940 the line has been owned by Brighton Corporation.

Running close behind the Snowdon Mountain Railway in the longevity stakes is the **Groudle Glen Railway**, a short 2-foot-gauge railway on the Isle of Man that opened in 1896. The glen, 3 miles to the north of Douglas, was a popular tourist attraction and its owners needed some form of transport to carry visitors to a small zoo they had opened in a cove nearby.

The **Romney, Hythe & Dymchurch Railway** is undoubtedly the ultimate trainset, with scale locomotives, double track, signalling, and a main line in 15-inch gauge. Located on the Kentish coast not far

LEFT The Snowdon Mountain Railway, opened in 1895, is 4½ miles long, with a gradient as steep as 1 in 5.5 above Clogwyn. Two viaducts carry the line out of Llanberis onto the mountain. Now owned by a Channel Islands trust which operates other tourist attractions, it has four operational steam locomotives and four diesel locomotives.

Following the introduction of new carriages in 2013, one of the displaced vehicles was rebodied in a style that reflected the original vehicles when new. In this form it is being used on a 'heritage steam experience' with a steam locomotive. No 2 *Enid* was being used to demonstrate the carriage on 31 May 2013. *Author*

RIGHT Magnus Volk opened a quarter-mile-long 2-foot-gauge electric railway, running on 50v DC, along the front at Brighton in 1883. The following year it was extended by half a mile, re-gauged to 2ft 9in and had its power supply increased to 160v DC. A third rail was added to supply current in 1886, when the gauge was also reduced by half an inch. Over the years it has been extended and truncated, reaching its present 1¼-mile length in 1998. The line has been owned by Brighton Corporation since 1940.

RIGHT Opened in 1896, the Groudle Glen Railway was closed in 1962 and became derelict. Its restoration was started by the Isle of Man Steam Railway Supporters Association in 1982.

Passing the site of the later locomotive shed, Bagnall 2-4-0T *Sea Lion* leaves Lehn Coan and heads of Sea Lion Rocks. A second locomotive, named *Polar Bear*, was obtained in 1905; both survive. Published two years after the railway was opened in 1896, this view shows how the glen appeared before it became overgrown by trees. The Groudle Hotel, a station on the 3-foot-gauge Manx Electric Railway, is on the skyline.

from Eastbourne, it runs alongside a military canal, across Romney Marsh and through an expanse of shingle at Dungeness; it even had an exchange siding with the Southern Railway at New Romney. It is also a light railway, constructed at the behest of Captain J. E. P. Howey, opened between New Romney and Hythe in 1927, and extended to Dungeness in 1928, making 13½ miles in total. Initially there were seven steam locomotives, five 4-6-2s and two 4-8-2s based on Gresley designs for the LNER. In 1931 two Canadian Pacific-type 4-6-2s were added to the fleet.

Howey, a millionaire property owner, intended the railway to be a common carrier, but the anticipated mineral traffic was short-lived. However, the railway did, and still does, find a ready market with holidaymakers. It was taken over by the military during the war and suffered somewhat, the second track to Dungeness not being reinstated. Unfortunately Howey saw no future for the railway after his death in 1963 and made no provision for it. It was sold by his widow and changed hands again, suffering from a lack of maintenance and investment. It was 'rescued' by an enthusiast-led group in 1973 and thrives with the support of its shareholders and supporters' association.

The line has seen many improvements, including the addition of new locomotives, steam and diesel, to the fleet. The stations are undergoing a programme of enhancements and a new locomotive repair workshop has been built. Since 1977 school days have been enlivened by the operation of trains run for pupils attending a school in New Romney.

The revival of the Talyllyn and Festiniog railways in the 1950s was responsible for the expansion in the use of narrow gauge railways on new sites as tourist attractions, mostly driven by enthusiasts but in some cases devised as commercial ventures.

Some were established on the trackbeds of recently closed standard gauge lines, starting with the **Bala Lake Railway** (Rheilffordd Llyn Tegid in Welsh) on the trackbed of a part of the Bala & Dolgelly Railway, one of the nominally independent railways that made the route between Ruabon and Dolgellau, linking the GWR to the Cambrian Railways. The BDR was opened in 1868 and taken over by the GWR in 1877. Its key feature was the 4½-mile section east of the small village of Llanuwchllyn, where it ran alongside Bala Lake, Llyn Tegid, the largest natural lake in Wales. After the railway was closed by

RIGHT The Romney, Hythe & Dymchurch Railway's owner, Captain J. E. P. Howey, was a man with connections who understood the value of publicity. No surprise then that on 5 August 1926 the railway, still incomplete, played host to a visit by HRH the Duke of York, later King George VI, accompanied by the LNER's chief mechanical engineer, Nigel Gresley. When the train left New Romney, the Duke and Howey rode on the engine while Gresley sat in the tender. The railway was opened on 16 July 1927.

RIGHT Two two-cylinder 'Pacifics' had been ordered by Howey's friend, Count Louis Zborowski, in 1924, Howey taking over the order after Zborowski died in November of that year. In 1925 the order was increased by a third two-cylinder and two three-cylinder 'Pacifics' and two 4-8-2s, which were delivered in 1926. Intended for short-lived freight trains, the 4-8-2s saw little use until pointwork had been renewed enabling them to access all lines.

DUNGENESS LIGHTHOUSE, ROMNEY HYTHE & DYMCHURCH LIGHT RAILWAY

LEFT Two Canadian-style 'Pacifics' were delivered by the Yorkshire Engine Company in 1931. No 9 *Dr Syn* is seen on the former Lynton & Barnstaple Railway turntable that Howey bought in the auction after that railway was closed in 1935.

RIGHT No 2 *Northern Chief* passes through New Romney with a train of ballast wagons on 25 July 1947. Howey's ambition that his railway should carry freight as well as passengers was not fulfilled. *J. C. Flemons*

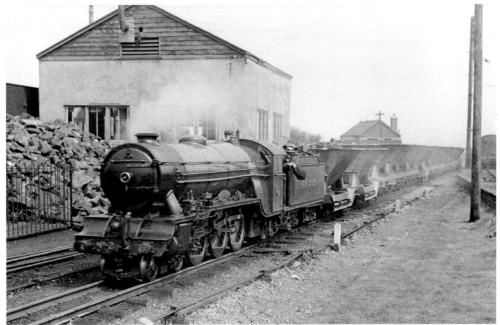

RIGHT At Hythe the RHDR runs parallel to the military canal, a Napoleonic defence. No 8 *Hurricane* was passing when photographed on 11 August 1954. *H. Buck*

LEFT The extension from New Romney to Dungeness was opened in 1928, and the double track continued for the 6 miles from New Romney, terminating in a large 'balloon' loop that eliminated the need for a turntable. Much of the route was across a sparsely inhabited shingle beach, the terminus being dominated by the lighthouse. Most of it has been built up over the post-war years and at the terminus the dominant features now are the Dungeness nuclear power stations that opened in 1965 and 1983/85. *Sport & General*

LEFT Seen on shed at New Romney on 15 May 2004 is the RHDR's first loco, 4-6-2 No 1 *Green Goddess*, built by Davey, Paxman at Colchester. Like six other RHDR locos, it was designed by Henry Greenly in the style of the Gresley-designed 'Pacifics' that ran on the LNER. Dual-braked originally, the air brake was removed when the railway standardised on vacuum in 1927. Notice the protectors fitted to the buffers to preserve their polished surfaces. *Author*

LEFT Hythe turntable is the location of this portrait of 4-8-2 No 5 *Hercules* on a rather unseasonal 1 October 2005. *Author*

BELOW Seen on the coal road at Hythe on 11 June 2011, 4-6-2 No 10 *Dr Syn* was celebrating its 80th anniversary a year after it had undergone a complete overhaul. *Author*

LEFT 4-6-2 No 11 *Black Prince* was built by Krupp for a German exhibition railway in 1937. It was bought by the RHDR in 1976; two other locomotives built at the same time are based at Bressingham in Norfolk. *Author*

LEFT Howey obtained this Krauss 0-4-0T to use on construction trains in 1926. Named *The Bug*, it was sold in the early 1930s, finishing up at Bellevue Park, Belfast, named *Jean*. Sold for scrap in 1950, it was discovered in a scrapyard in 1972 and purchased by the RHDR's chairman, W. H. McAlpine. Restored to service in 1977, it is now a regular participant during special events and was photographed arriving at Hythe on 13 May 2006. *Author*

BELOW Howey's favourite loco, No 8 *Hurricane*, was photographed at Dungeness on 15 May 2004. *Author*

British Railways in 1965, Merionethshire County Council bought the land, leasing this part to the BLR Company for development as a tourist railway. The 2-foot-gauge railway was opened in stages between 1972 and 1976.

In 1975 the railway became the home of Dinorwic quarry Hunslet 0-4-0ST *Maid Marian* in the face of some doubt about its capability on the line's 1 in 70 Ddolfawr bank with a loaded passenger train, but it showed its metal and was followed by *Holy War*, *Alice*, *George B* and *Winifred*. The last two are being restored. In 2012 *Winifred* was returned to Wales after 47 years of exile in the USA, unchanged from the day that it left Penrhyn quarry. The combination of the lake, fine views in the Snowdonia National Park and quarry Hunslets has proved to be a winning one for the Bala Lake Railway.

ABOVE Llanuwchllyn station was built by the Bala & Dolgelly Railway, opened in 1868. The station canopy was obtained from Aberdovey, having been previously at Pwllheli. The signal box and its frame are original but the station's signals are of Lancashire & Yorkshire Railway origin, the BLR's founder, George Barnes, being an enthusiast for that railway's equipment. The diesel-hydraulic locomotive, *Meirionnydd*, was built for the railway by Severn Lamb in 1973. Used on off-peak passenger trains, it has been out of service for several years requiring a replacement engine. *Author*

BELOW Passing a fine array of signals, ex-Dinorwic Hunslet 0-4-0ST *Holy War* arrives at Llangower, the BLR's main intermediate station. *Holy War* shares the roster with ex-Dinorwic Hunslet 0-4-0ST *Maid Marian*, and has been running on the BLR since 1978. *Author*

ABOVE Bala Lake, Llyn Tegid in Welsh, was the largest natural body of water in Wales until Thomas Telford increased its capacity to provide extra water to the Ellesmere Canal in the early 19th century; the River Dee passes through it. Four miles long and up to a mile wide, it is popular with sailors and windsurfers.

The third ex-Dinorwic Hunslet 0-4-0ST based at the Bala Lake Railway is *Alice*, which retains a more traditional appearance. Based at the BLR from 1977, its reconstruction was completed at the Ffestiniog Railway's Boston Lodge works in 1994. It then worked at the Leighton Buzzard Railway in Bedfordshire until October 2003, when it returned to Llanuwchllyn. It has been known to be operated in less than clement weather. *Author*

LEFT The fifth Hunslet 0-4-0ST to be based at the BLR is *Winifred*, one of seven Penrhyn quarry locomotives exported to the USA and Canada in the 1960s. After many years in an air-conditioned store in Tennessee it returned to Wales on 28 April 2012, looking much the same as when it left in 1965. The photograph shows it with *Alice*, shortly after it had been unloaded. Restoration was started in 2013. *Author*

In South Wales, the **Brecon Mountain Railway** has been built on a 5½-mile section of the former Brecon & Merthyr Railway, which closed in 1962. The section concerned starts at Pant, in the Brecon Beacons National Park, north of Merthyr Tydfil and close to the A465 Heads of the Valleys main road.

After more than six years of planning, and many more acquiring equipment, construction was started in 1978. The original Pant station site not being available, an adjoining field was purchased and the line's headquarters developed there. In the workshop the railway has built its own carriages and restored several locomotives, including the manufacture of several boilers. The restoration of a Baldwin 2-6-0 as a 2-6-2 should be completed in 2015, and the production of components for two more Baldwin-style locomotives has been started.

Services started to Pontsticill, alongside Taf Fechan reservoir (2 miles) in 1980, and were extended to Dolygaer in 1984 and Torpantau in 2014. The original motive power was a Hunslet 0-4-0ST named *Sybil*, which hauled a single carriage. The Hunslet was replaced by Jung 0-6-2WTT *Graf Schwerin-Löwitz*, which was obtained from the former East Germany, and Baldwin 4-6-0 No 24, obtained from South Africa. *Sybil* and two other locomotives have been restored and are displayed in a small museum at Pontsticill.

ABOVE Jung 0-6-2WTT *Graf Schwerin-Löwitz* waits to leave the Brecon Mountain Railway's Pant headquarters, just north of Merthyr Tydfil, on 16 April 1995. The building, which bears some resemblance to a Welsh chapel from the front, accommodates the railway's offices, a café, souvenir shop and workshop. On the right overgrown spoil heaps hint at the area's industrial past. *Author*

RIGHT When *Graf Schwerin-Löwitz* was withdrawn while a new boiler was built for it over the winter of 1992/93, the Vale of Rheidol Railway's 2-6-2T No 9 *Prince of Wales* was brought in to work the season's Santa trains. At the time the BMR was managing the VRR, and No 9 had recently been overhauled at Pant. With Pontsticill reservoir and the Brecon Beacons as a backdrop, No 9 returns to Pant on 20 December 1992. *Author*

RIGHT Built in 1930, this Baldwin 4-6-2 operated on the Eastern Province Cement Company's branch line at Port Elizabeth in South Africa, being badly damaged after it ran away in 1973. In 1974 it was imported to the UK, being stored initially at Llanberis. After many years of effort it was restored and entered service on the BMR in 1997. *Author*

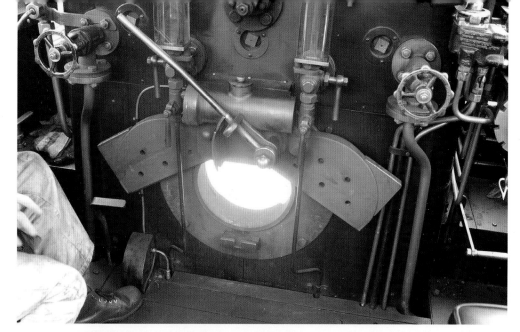

LEFT During its 10-year boiler overhaul in 2008/09 the Baldwin was converted from burning oil to burn coal, receiving an air-operated firehole door in the process. It was demonstrated for the author on 20 August 2009. *Author*

LEFT The Brecon Mountain Railway's workshop is amongst the most comprehensive on a British narrow gauge railway. Seen on 10 April 2014 is an 1897-built Baldwin 2-6-0 imported from Brazil which is being restored as a 2-6-2. *Author*

BELOW The BMR's long-awaited extension to Torpantau was opened without ceremony on 1 April 2014. On a dull 10 April the railway's diesel locomotive made a rare substitution for steam, seen leaving Dolygaer with a much lighter load than normal. *Author*

ABOVE Lt-Cdr Roy Francis, the Wells & Walsingham Light Railway's founder and proprietor, waters the 10¼-inch-gauge line's first Garratt, *Norfolk Hero*, at Wells on 29 May 1994. The locomotive was commissioned to suit the railway's requirements. *Author*

RIGHT A second Garratt was built in 2010. Although incomplete, it was named *Norfolk Heroine* by the Countess of Leicester on 16 October. Known as the 'Norfolk heroine', Edith Cavell, the nurse who was executed during the First World War, was born in Norfolk. *Author*

BELOW RIGHT *Norfolk Hero* was named after Horatio Nelson, the Napoleonic sailor born in Norfolk who died as he won victory at the Battle of Trafalgar in 1805. One of the disadvantages of building narrow gauge railways on standard gauge formations is demonstrated here on 29 May 1994. Those who rode in standard gauge trains on this route would have seen the North Sea, a view that is lost to those who travel closer to the ground. *Author*

At 4 miles long, the 10¼-inch- gauge **Wells & Walsingham Light Railway** must be the smallest public railway in the world. Located on the trackbed of the former Great Eastern Railway branch from Dereham, it links the seaside resort of Wells with Walsingham, a large village known for its religious shrines.

The railway is the passion of Lieutenant-Commander Roy Francis. Having built the 1-mile-long beach railway in Wells, also 10¼-inch gauge, in 1976, he started on the Wells & Walsingham line, opening it in 1982.

Apart from emergencies, the WWLR has been entirely Garratt operated since 1987, a claim that not even the Welsh Highland Railway can match. Designed and built for the railway by Neil Simkins, 2-6-0+0-6-2T *Norfolk Hero* is the master of the task set for it, regularly hauling loads of up to 76 passengers. In 2011 it was joined by *Norfolk Heroine*, another 2-6-0+0-6-2T Garratt.

Set on the border of Devon and Cornwall and opened in 1983, the **Launceston Steam Railway** was built on the trackbed of the former London & South Western Railway line that ran through the Kensey valley en route between Halwill Junction and Padstow, once the haunt of Bulleid 'Light Pacifics' and loaded holiday trains. At first operated as an out-and-back 2-mile ride westwards from Launceston, a half-mile extension to New Mills opened in 1995 gave it a purpose, exchanging traffic with a farm park.

The standard gauge station site having been redeveloped, the LSR's Launceston station is located on the site of the town's former gas works, which was also on the site of an Augustinian priory. The station canopy, given to the railway by West Devon District Council, was

ABOVE The Launceston Steam Railway's carriages are stored out of season under the platform canopy at Launceston station, as seen on 4 February 2001. *Author*

originally at Tavistock North station. Rails on the platform are used to store the carriages during the winter.

Services are operated by Hunslet 0-4-0STs, *Lilian* from Penrhyn, *Covertcoat* from Dinorwic, and *Dorothea* from the Dorothea quarry in the Nantlle valley. *Velinheli*, also based on the railway, is another Dinorwic loco. The LSR's passenger rolling stock is quite quirky, using Torrington & Marland Railway and Manx Electric Railway prototypes for inspiration.

RIGHT In one of the most industrial settings to be found on a British narrow gauge tourist railway, Launceston Steam Railway proprietor Nigel Bowman coals Hunslet 0-4-0STT *Covertcoat* on 6 September 1995. *Author*

LEFT Viewed on 6 August 1995, Hunslet 0-4-0ST *Lilian* normally lives in this little shed with a very ornate façade. *Author*

RIGHT Hunslet 0-4-0ST *Dorothea* calls at New Mills, the LSR's western terminus, on 8 April 2012. *Author*

RIGHT Seeing the tracks on the platform on 24 May 1998, a visiting driver had to take Hunslet 0-4-0ST *Velinheli* up just to prove that it could be done. Hunslet 0-4-0ST *Lilla* is hiding behind *Covertcoat*. *Author*

ABOVE Resident at the Teifi Valley Railway since 1987, Hunslet 0-4-0ST *Alan George* was for many years the railway's only steam locomotive. The width of the former broad gauge formation is clearly evident in this view of a train returning to Henllan on 25 May 1992. *Author*

TOP RIGHT In 1996 *Alan George* was joined by Kerr, Stuart 0-6-2T *Sgt. Murphy*. Initially on loan, the locomotive was later purchased by the railway. The pair are seen together at Henllan on 31 May 1997. *Alan George* had been fitted with a cab the previous winter. *Author*

CENTRE RIGHT The 800m extension to Pont Goch, where the line originally crossed the Afon Teifi, was opened on 1 April 2006. On that occasion *Sgt. Murphy* was photographed while running round. The river bridge had been demolished in 1994 when it had become unsafe. *Author*

BOTTOM RIGHT The guard gives the 'right away' and joins the train as it leaves the new Henllan platform on 20 August 2009. *Alan George*'s cab had been removed two years earlier. *Author*

Deep in rural Carmarthenshire, the **Teifi Valley Railway** has been built on the trackbed of the former Great Western Railway broad gauge branch that served the small market town of Newcastle Emlyn. In 1854 the line's original promoters intended to connect Carmarthen with Cardigan but, as with so many similar rural railway schemes, it proved impossible to raise sufficient finance and construction stopped at Llandysul. Under GWR control, the 7-mile extension to Newcastle Emlyn started in 1885 and was finished ten years later. Passenger services were withdrawn in 1952 and goods in 1973.

A local group bought the 10-mile trackbed from Pencader Junction to Newcastle Emlyn and construction of the 2-foot-gauge TVR started from Henllan in 1983, the first section opening in 1985. The line was extended westwards to Pont Goch in 2006, and the platform at Henllan was moved eastwards in 2009, creating a 2-mile route. At Pont Goch the Afon Teifi requires bridging before the line can be extended further towards Newcastle Emlyn.

Passenger accommodation is in carriages built in-house, and trains are hauled by Hunslet 0-4-0ST *Alan George* or Kerr, Stuart 0-6-2T *Sgt. Murphy*.

Development of the **Bure Valley Railway** in Norfolk was an initiative of Broadlands District Council, which identified the 9-mile route of the former Great Eastern Railway between Wroxham and Aylsham as suitable for a tourist railway and footpath. The termini are market towns, Aylsham being particularly attractive, while Wroxham is on the Norfolk Broads and still has the benefit of being served by the train service that operates between Norwich and Sheringham.

The line had been built as the Aylsham extension of the East Norfolk Railway, opened in 1879 to Buxton and in 1880 to Aylsham. In common with many other railways, it was built cheaply, following the contours where possible. Its route through the Bure valley took it through open countryside, serving scattered communities. Absorbed by the Great Eastern Railway in 1881, the ENR had always effectively been controlled by that company. Closure to passengers in 1952 pre-dated the Beeching era by 11 years, although the local goods service continued until 1974 and through goods to Lenwade and Norwich until 1982. The track was lifted in 1984.

Not having the funds to complete the development itself, the council purchased the land from British Rail and leased it to a company formed to construct the footpath and build and operate the 15-inch-gauge railway. The English Tourist Board and the Department of the Environment made grants of £2½ million to pay for structural repairs, while the railway company bought the land for the terminal stations. The 200-yard tunnel under Aylsham bypass cost £300,000.

When the railway was opened in 1990 steam locomotives were hired from the Romney, Hythe & Dymchurch Railway. The railway company's parent went into liquidation in January 1991, placing the railway's future in doubt. A new company was registered in that year and over the next few years three more owners ran the line, eventually finding a way to develop its performance with volunteer support. The present management took control in 2001.

The collapse of the original company caused something of a locomotive crisis for the BVR because the RHDR locomotives were no

ABOVE When it opened in 1990 the Bure Valley Railway hired two locomotives from the Romney, Hythe & Dymchurch Railway. With the cycle track alongside, 4-6-2 No 9 *Winston Churchill* was photographed heading towards Wroxham.

BELOW From 1994 the BVR has been reliant on these two half-size Indian 'ZB' 2-6-2s, Nos 6 and 7, now named *Blickling Hall* and *Spitfire* respectively. Originally intended to be exact copies of the prototypes, the flags lasted as long as it took for them to get dirty and the cabside shutters on No 6 did not last much longer. When photographed on 29 May 1994 No 7 was being commissioned, No 6 having been delivered a few weeks earlier. *Author*

longer available. However, locomotives were found and the railway carried on. In 1994 two new half-size 'ZB' 2-6-2 locomotives were delivered. The prototype was a standard design for Indian 2ft 6in-gauge railways, and has proved to be ideal on the BVR. Two 2-6-2Ts with different profiles but to the same underlying design were delivered in 1996 and 1999.

RIGHT A third locomotive was built in 1997, No 8, a 2-6-2T using the 'ZB' undercarriage with the outline of one of the Vale of Rheidol Railway 2-6-2Ts. It was erected in the BVR's workshop. An oil burner when new, No 8 was converted to coal when oil prices increased. It was named *John of Gaunt* in 2014. It was photographed with Nos 7 and 6 on 16 April 1999. The locomotive on the right was a variant of the 'ZB' design, having a 2-6-4 wheel arrangement, and had just been unloaded. No 10 in the BVR fleet, it represented a County Donegal Railway prototype but never entered service in this form. *Author*

LEFT When No 10 proved to be unsuitable it was rebuilt as a Leek & Manifold Light Railway locomotive, entering service in 2003 as No 9 *Mark Timothy*. It was photographed on 9 October 2005 crossing a minor road near Aylsham. *Author*

LEFT An unusual working took place on 21 May 2000 when James Waterfield's replica of Sir Arthur Heywood's 0-6-0T *Ursula* was run with his replica Heywood dining car serving dinner to guests. The original *Ursula* entered service on the Duke of Westminster's Eaton Railway in 1916, and was scrapped in 1942. The menu comprised baked Norfolk gammon, coronation chicken, green salad, tomato vinaigrette and new potato salad accompanied by chilled Piesporter and followed by lemon syllabub and coffee and mints. The train was photographed at Brampton loop, 3 miles from Aylsham. *Author*

LEFT The token is handed in at Alston signal box on the South Tynedale Railway on 22 July 2013. The locomotive is a Henschel 0-4-0WT named *Thomas Edmondson* after the inventor of the card ticket issuing system used by railways throughout the world. He started his railway career nearby, on the Newcastle & Carlisle Railway. The signal box, which controls the level crossing access to the car park, was obtained from Ainderby, on the North Eastern Railway's Redmire branch. *Author*

BELOW Another Henschel based at the South Tynedale Railway is 0-4-0T *Helen Kathryn*, seen here on Gilderdale Viaduct, one of the 35 listed structures on the 17-mile route between Alston and Haltwhistle, on 4 August 2002. *Author*

BOTTOM The Polish Chrzanów 0-6-0WTT *Naklø* runs light engine on the then unopened part of the railway beyond Gilderdale on 21 September 1996. *Author*

High in the Pennines, literally as well as geographically, the **South Tynedale Railway** has its origins in a branch of the Newcastle & Carlisle Railway. The valley of the South Tyne was a well-established industrial area, with collieries and lead mines, when railways came to the area in the 19th century. Construction of the 14-mile branch between Haltwhistle and Alston was started in 1849 and completed in 1852. Gradients as steep as 1 in 56 lifted the line 500 feet, and nine viaducts carried it across the South Tyne.

Withdrawal of goods services was completed by 1965 and the passenger service was withdrawn in 1976. Failing to raise the money to buy the branch from BR, the preservation society decided on a narrow gauge scheme, adopting the 2-foot gauge. Services at Alston started in 1983 and an extension to Gilderdale followed in 1987. Services were extended to Kirkhaugh (2¼ miles) in 1999, and to Lintley (3¼ miles) in 2012. Work is in progress to extend the line to Slaggyford, another 1¼ miles and the limit of the existing powers. The railway has ambitions to extend to Haltwhistle in due course.

ABOVE During a later overhaul, *Naklø* had its tanks removed, as shown in this picture of it running round at Kirkhaugh on 4 August 2002. *Author*

LEFT *Thomas Edmondson* arrives at Lintley, the South Tynedale Railway's terminus since 2012. The train now includes a Romanian carriage that is wheelchair-accessible and one of the ex-Sierra Leone Railway carriages previously owned by the Welshpool & Llanfair Light Railway, which has been converted into a buffet car. Trains heading back to Alston face a 1 in 56 gradient. *Author*

LEFT The STR intends to restore the line to Slaggyford, the limit of its existing powers, by 2016. The line will then be 4½ miles long. *Author*

ABOVE A prominent feature in the Kirklees Light Railway's landscape is the mast of Emley Moor TV transmitting station, about 3 miles from the railway's Clayton West headquarters. The design of *Hawk* was based on a Kitson-Meyer articulated locomotive built by Barclay for export to Chile. Photographed on 9 September 2012, the signal alongside does not control rail traffic but reminds users of the road below of the railway's existence. *Author*

RIGHT *Badger*, an 0-6-4ST developed from the Kerr, Stuart 'Tattoo' class, stands on the turntable outside the engine shed at Clayton West. The Midland Railway station building was to be demolished 'because it was in the wrong place'. *Author*

BELOW RIGHT Based on an Avonside design, *Owl* is driven by gears. The photograph was taken on 9 September 2012. *Author*

The **Kirklees Light Railway** is targeted at families from Yorkshire's metropolitan areas but there is much to commend it to the enthusiast. The 3½-mile branch was built by the Lancashire & Yorkshire Railway and opened in 1879. Its main traffic was coal from its one intermediate station, Skelmanthorpe, and Park Mill colliery at Clayton West. The colliery traffic ended in 1970, passenger services lasting until 1983; the track was lifted in 1986. A Light Railway Order was obtained for the 15-inch-gauge railway in 1991 and the line was extended from Clayton West to Shelley in stages, being completed in 1996. All the stock, locomotives and carriages, was built by its founder, the late Brian Taylor. Features include the 511-yard Shelley Woodhouse Tunnel, the longest on any 15-inch-gauge railway, and views of the distinctive Emley Moor TV transmitter mast, at 1,084 feet high the tallest freestanding structure in the UK. The nature of the wildlife to be seen from the trains is reflected in the locomotives' names. The railway changed hands in 2005, and its operation is supported by a committed team of volunteers.

RIGHT A train arrives at the Newlands Inn terminus of the Golden Valley Light Railway on 23 May 1998. The sharp curve at the rear of the train was straightened out in 2012. *Author*

BELOW *Pearl 2*, the GVLR's first resident working steam loco, returns to Butterley on 16 August 2003. The locomotive subsequently changed hands and was renamed *Joan*. *Author*

ABOVE Steam is raised on 7 July 2007, when the railway marked the completion of the running shed and workshop. *Author*

BELOW This is the Ashover Light Railway carriage as it was received, seen on 25 August 2005. At the time of publication its restoration has just been completed. *Author*

The 2-foot-gauge **Golden Valley Light Railway** is an adjunct to the Midland Railway Centre at Butterley, near Ripley in Derbyshire, and gives visitors the option of a ride into an area not seen from the standard gauge line, now protected as a country park. Development of the railway was started in the 1980s and it now extends for nearly a mile from Butterley Park to the former Newlands Inn at Golden Valley. A part of the route was originally the trackbed of the Butterley Company's pre-1834 plateway between Butterley and Codnor Park, and another crosses a disused reservoir that fed the Cromford Canal.

Most of the railway's equipment has been obtained from industry, particularly Derbyshire and Nottinghamshire collieries. Appropriately, the passenger 'carriages' are modified colliery manriders that were used to carry miners underground. In 1997 the GVLR became one of the first railways to be authorised by a 1992 Transport & Works Act order. Most trains are hauled by an unusual 0-4-0 with an inverted saddle tank, which was built by the late Allen Civil. The railway's volunteers are restoring an Orenstein & Koppel 0-4-0WT and a former Ashover Light Railway carriage.

In the 1950s enthusiasts who wanted to be involved with narrow gauge railways had to travel to Wales, not an easy journey from most parts in those pre-motorway days. In Lincolnshire a group got together and established the **Lincolnshire Coast Light Railway**, which opened in 1960. Using equipment gathered from various sources and on land leased from the local authority, a railway was built to serve holidaymakers at Humberston, near Cleethorpes, the first to be built and operated by enthusiasts on a greenfield site. Successful at first, it

was closed and dismantled in 1985, the stock being later moved to Skegness where a new railway is being developed with the same name.

BELOW The only steam locomotive to see regular service on the Lincolnshire Coast Light Railway was ex-Southam cement works Peckett 0-6-0ST *Jurassic*. At the time of publication it had last steamed during the Leighton Buzzard Railway's gala on 21 September 1986.

Enthusiast groups also took over industrial narrow gauge railways, at **Leighton Buzzard** (2-foot gauge, in 1968) and **Sittingbourne** (2ft 6in, 1969), establishing bases for the restoration and preservation of equipment, and operating public passenger services where there had been none before. A commercial group took over part of the 4-foot-gauge Padarn (slate) Railway at Llanberis and developed it as the 2-foot-gauge **Llanberis Lake Railway** tourist attraction from 1971.

RIGHT Three and a half miles long, the Leighton Buzzard Light Railway was built by sand quarry owners to carry their output to exchange sidings with the LNWR and was opened in 1919. The railway's use was in decline in the 1960s, when enthusiasts agreed to take over a 3-mile section and started a steam-worked passenger service in 1968. The railway's members have formed a small collection of steam locomotives and a much larger one of internal combustion machines. Seen leaving the main station at Page's Park on 26 May 2013 is Baldwin 4-6-0T No 778, built for the War Department in 1917. After the war it was used on an Indian sugar plantation until the 1980s. *Author*

ABOVE The Llanberis Lake Railway was opened in 1971/72, and 2 miles of its route is on the formation of the former 4-foot gauge Padarn Railway, running along the shore of Llyn Padarn. The half-mile extension between Gilfach Ddu and Llanberis, across the road from the Snowdon Mountain Railway, was opened in 2007. The railway owns three Hunslet 0-4-0STs that used to work in the Dinorwic slate quarries. *Dolbadarn* was photographed westbound on 6 July 2013; the summit of Snowdon is visible on the right. *Author*

BELOW Since it entered preservation in 1969, the Sittingbourne & Kemsley Light Railway has not had an easy time, struggling to attract visitors in an area that is not naturally attractive to tourists. Running through open countryside, the locality's industrial activity, past and present, is much in evidence. Kerr, Stuart 'Tattoo' 0-4-2ST *Leader* is seen heading for Sittingbourne on 27 May 2012, the first day of operations after five years of closure while a new lease was secured. *Author*

New railways have also been established in a clay pit (**West Lancashire Light Railway**, Hesketh Bank), a chalk pit (**Amberley Museum & Heritage Centre**, West Sussex), a colliery (**Apedale Heritage Centre**, Newcastle under Lyme), a slate mine (**Llechwedd**, Blaenau Ffestiniog), a granite quarry (**Threlkeld**, Cumbria), a lido (**Ruislip**), a brickworks (**Burlesdon**, Hampshire), a railway station (**Bickleigh**, Devon), a zoo (**Whipsnade**, Bedfordshire), the grounds of a stately home (**Longleat**, Wiltshire) and an open-air museum (**Beamish**, Northumbria), in gardens at **Bressingham**, Norfolk; **Bicton**, Devon, and **Exbury**, Hampshire, a garden centre (**Evesham**), farm parks at **Amerton**, Staffordshire, and **Burscough**, Lancashire, and waterworks at **Kew**, **Hampton**, **Leicester** and **Twyford**. This list is by no means complete.

ABOVE In 1967 six Southport schoolboys sowed the seeds for what became the West Lancashire Light Railway by acquiring some track and a pair of axles. One of the parents allowed them to use family-owned land around a disused claypit at Hesketh Bank. The youngsters went from strength to strength and built a railway nearly a mile long; they have also restored several steam locomotives. Seen on 10 August 2013 the locomotive is a Kerr, Stuart 'Joffre' 0-6-0WT, one of five that found a new use in a French quarry in 1930 and were repatriated to the UK in 1974 after many years out of use. Restoration was started in 1995 and completed in 2012. Another restored example is based at the Apedale Valley Light Railway in Staffordshire. *Author*

RIGHT Amberley Museum & Heritage Centre is located in an old chalk pit near Worthing, West Sussex. Until the 1960s the chalk was used in the production of lime and cement. The museum is home to an extensive industrial railway collection that comprises mostly narrow gauge-related exhibits. A demonstration railway assists in transporting visitors around the 34-acre site. Hauling the train on 13 July 2013 was Bagnall 0-4-0ST *Peter*, which originally worked at the Cliffe Hill quarry in Leicestershire. *Author*

ABOVE In Staffordshire, the Apedale Heritage Centre is home to the Moseley Railway Trust's Apedale Valley Light Railway. The site is that of a colliery near Newcastle under Lyme, which has been reclaimed as a country park. Opened in 2010, the first phase of a railway that will eventually be 1¼ miles long carries passengers and is usually steam-operated. The trust, however, has a large collection of internal combustion locomotives, some of which are demonstrated in an environment not dissimilar to that of many industrial railways of days gone by. This was the scene on 14 September 2014. *Author*

ABOVE Threlkeld granite quarry is in the Lake District, near Keswick; it closed in 1982, redevelopment as a tourist attraction started in 1992, and the construction of a railway to take visitors into the quarry was started circa 2001. Since it was returned to steam in 2010, most trains are hauled by Bagnall 0-4-0ST *Sir Tom*, already encountered in this book, which was restored on site. In July each year the quarry has a railway event with visiting locomotives. Here, on 27 July 2013, the Statfold Barn Railway's Hunslet 0-4-0ST *Sibyl Mary* is hauling the train with assistance from *Sir Tom* at the rear. *Author*

ABOVE At just half a mile long, the Devon Railway Centre's 2-foot-gauge railway demonstrates how a lot of railway can be packed into a small space. Based at the South Devon Railway's Bickleigh station, near Tiverton, the centre was opened in 1998. Orenstein & Koppel 0-4-0WT No 14 *Rebecca*, built in 1912, was imported from Argentina and restored in Devon over a period of eight years, entering service in July 2013. Here it catches the sun while on Santa train duty on 23 December 2013. *Author*

RIGHT First opened in 1970, the 2ft 6in-gauge Great Whipsnade Railway takes visitors on a 1½-mile journey through several animal enclosures in the Zoological Society of London's Whipsnade Zoo. Photographed on 26 May 2012, Kerr, Stuart 0-6-2T *Superior* was built for Bowater's, Sittingbourne, in 1920. *Author*

ABOVE Beamish, 'The Living Museum of the North', is 12 miles from Durham. Opened in 1971, the museum aims to demonstrate all aspects of life in the North East from 1820 to the 1950s, including various forms of transport. A recent development is the 2-foot-gauge industrial railway, which at the time of writing is demonstrated by the use of visiting steam locomotives. Taken on 14 April 2014, the photograph shows two Barclay 0-4-0Ts that formerly worked at the Granton gas works. No 5 arrived at Beamish on long-term loan from the National Museum of Scotland in January 2013 and may be restored at some future date. No 9 was paying a short visit to the museum and transporting the stone being used to demonstrate road building. In comparison with No 5, it shows a number of changes made while it was being used on the Groudle Glen Railway in the 1990s. *Author*

LEFT *Isabel* is a Bagnall 0-4-0ST that was supplied to the Cliffe Hill quarry in 1897. Out of service in 1946, in 1953 the Bagnall company bought it back to display as a memorial to the 3,000 locomotives built in the works at Stafford and to the men who designed and built them. After the works closed in 1961 it was put on display in Victoria Park, Stafford, where it stayed until 1984. Restoration was started in 1985 and completed in 1991. For a base, the Staffordshire Narrow Gauge Railway Society, which had overhauled the loco, found premises at Amerton Farm, near Uttoxeter, where a farm park and garden centre already operated. The first phase of a railway was opened in 1992; a complete circuit 1 mile long was opened in 2001. Since 1992 the Amerton Railway has formed a collection of locomotives built in Staffordshire. *Author*

RIGHT The Metropolitan Water Board Railway was a rare example of a narrow gauge industrial railway constructed using the powers of an Act of Parliament. A 2-foot-gauge railway serving the board's works at Hampton, Kempton and Sunbury and a wharf on the Thames, a system less than 3 miles long, commenced operations in 1915. Three 0-4-2T locomotives were built to the board's designs by Kerr, Stuart. Modernisation, new techniques and the war brought the railway to an end in the 1940s. Revival proposals were first made in 1999, and the Metropolitan Water Board Railway Society was established in 2002. Under the title of the Hampton & Kempton Waterworks Railway, the first section of new railway, the Hanworth loop, was opened on 17 May 2013, when the photograph was taken. The locomotive is a Kerr, Stuart 'Wren' 0-4-0ST, construction of which was started at the London Museum of Water & Steam at Kew Bridge and completed by the Hunslet Engine Company in 2009. It has since returned to Kew Bridge. It is named *Thomas Wicksteed*, once engineer for five of the nine London water companies. *Author*

The spirit of Sir Arthur Heywood and his campaign for 15 inches as the minimum practical gauge is continued at several locations, particularly at Perrygrove, Gloucestershire, where a short railway packs many features into a small space.

ABOVE Set in the Forest of Dean, the 15-inch-gauge Perrygrove Railway is as good a demonstration of Sir Arthur Heywood's 'minimum gauge' principles as can be found, comprising a three-quarter-mile-long railway with sharp curves and steep gradients in a small space. On 22 September 2012 tokens are being exchanged between the drivers of the replica 0-6-0T *Ursula*, completed in 1999, and 2-6-2T *Lydia*, designed and built by Alan Keef Ltd for the railway and delivered in 2008. *Author*

A development of the Heywood concept occurred with the conversion of the 15-inch-gauge Fairbourne Railway to 12¼-inch gauge in 1986, demonstrating that it is still possible to seat two adults side-by-side. Developed commercially by the Exmoor Steam Railway in Devon, this has become a popular gauge for private railways. In the New Forest, the **Exbury Garden Railway** is an example of this gauge being used to its maximum.

ABOVE The capacity of a 12¼in gauge railway is demonstrated by this view of the Exbury Garden Railway at Exbury Central station on 13 August 2011. Taking a 1¼ mile route through 100 acres of gardens, the railway was opened in 2001. *Mariloo* is a 2-6-2 built by the Exmoor Steam Railway in 2008. The railway also has two 0-6-2Ts, *Rosemary* and *Naomi*, built at Exmoor in 2001 and 2002 respectively. *Author*

Private railways of 2-foot gauge were first brought to public attention when the Reverend E. R. ('Teddy') Boston built the **Cadeby Light Railway** at his rectory in Leicestershire. Opened in 1963, less than 100 yards long and regularly opened to the public until it was closed in 2005, it demonstrated that even in small spaces narrow gauge railways could be fun to operate and attractive to the public. Others have taken the idea further, and three that have regular public open days are the **Bredgar & Wormshill Light Railway** (near Sittingbourne, Kent), the **Beeches Light Railway** (near Banbury, Oxfordshire) and the **Statfold Barn Railway** (near Tamworth, Staffordshire).

ABOVE The vision of the Rev E. R. ('Teddy') Boston, the Cadeby Light Railway was the first to be built in what might be called a domestic setting, running round a rectory garden. From 1963 until 2005 it was regularly opened to the public. It became synonymous with its resident Bagnall 0-4-0ST *Pixie*, seen on 15 May 1999, 80 years after it was built, with members of the Narrow Gauge Railway Society. *Author*

ABOVE LEFT Established in 1974, the Bredgar & Wormshill Light Railway is another short railway, less than a mile long, on private property in Kent. It is open to the public several times a year, and is home to a small collection of steam locomotives, mostly obtained from overseas, which have been restored to a high standard, and is noted for features that include a turntable and manicured lawns. Seen on 28 October 2012, No 9 *Limpopo* is a Fowler 0-6-0WT built in 1930 for the Sena sugar estate in Mozambique. Returned to the UK in 1998, restoration at Bredgar started in 2000 and was completed in 2003. *Author*

LEFT The Beeches Light Railway takes its inspiration from the Darjeeling Himalayan Railway, being the base for the only DHR 'B' class 0-4-0ST to leave India, 1889-built No 19. Set in 3 acres in Oxfordshire, the 600-yard line describes an oval route around its owner's house, incorporating gradients as steep as 1 in 40 and 1 in 22, a minimum radius of 80 feet and crossovers that enable trains to take a figure-of-eight route if required. No 19 usually hauls replicas of two DHR carriages built at the Ffestiniog Railway's Boston Lodge works in 2003/04. *Author*

BELOW LEFT In just a few years the Statfold Barn Railway, located just outside Tamworth in Staffordshire, has had a significant impact on the preservation and restoration of narrow gauge locomotives. On a 1,500-acre farm, the railway comprises three lines, two of them 1½ miles long, one of them mixed 2-foot/2ft 6in-gauge. Locomotives that look like wrecks have been imported from around the world and restored to working order, often with new boilers, within a year or two. Three public open days held each year can attract up to 1,000 visitors to see more than a dozen locomotives in steam. Seen on 29 March 2013 on the garden railway, the first on the site, Hunslet 0-4-0ST *Jack Lane* is one of three locomotives built in the SBR's own workshops. *Author*

Bibliography

Boyd, James I. C. *The Schull & Skibbereen Railway* (Oakwood Press, 1999)

Boyd, J. I. C. *Talyllyn Railway* (Wild Swan, 1988)

Begley, Joe & Flanders, Steve *Ireland's Narrow Gauge Railways – a reference handbook* (Oakwood Press, 2012)

Bridges, A. (ed) *Industrial Locomotives of Scotland* (Industrial Railway Society, 1976)

Brown, G. A., Prideaux, J. D. C. & Radcliffe, H. G. *The Lynton & Barnstaple Railway* (Atlantic Transport Publishers, 1996)

Cartwright, Ralph L. *The Welshpool & Llanfair* (RailRomances, 2002)

Cooksey, Laurie A. *The Rye & Camber Tramway – a centenary history* (Plateway Press, 1995)

Crombleholme, Roger *The County Donegal Railways Companion* (Midland Publishing, 2005)

Davies, W. J. K. *The Ravenglass & Eskdale Railway* (Atlantic Transport Publishers, 2000)

Fairlie, R. F. *The Battle of the Gauges renewed – Railways or No Railways* (Effingham Wilson, 1872)

Gratton, Bob & Band, Stuart R. *The Ashover Light Railway* (Wild Swan, 1989)

Gratton, Bob *The Leek & Manifold Light Railway* (RCL Publications, 2005)

Green, C. C. *The Vale of Rheidol Light Railway* (Wild Swan, 1986)

Guerin, Michael *The Lartigue Listowel & Ballybunion Railway* (Lartigue Centenary Committee, 1988)

Hartley, K. E. & Ingham, P. *The Sand Hutton Light Railway* (RCL Publications, 2013)

Hateley, Roger (comp) *Industrial Railways and Locomotives of South Western England* (Industrial Railway Society, 2012)

Holmes, Alan *Talyllyn Revived – the story of the world's first railway preservation society* (Talyllyn Railway Co, 2009)

Jenkins, Stanley C. *The Cork, Blackrock & Passage Railway* (Oakwood Press, 2nd edition, 1993)

Johnson, Peter *An Illustrated History of the Festiniog Railway* (Oxford Publishing Co, 2007)

An Illustrated History of the Great Western Narrow Gauge [Corris Railway, Vale of Rheidol Light Railway, Welshpool & Llanfair Light Railway] (Oxford Publishing Co, 2011)

An Illustrated History of the Welsh Highland Railway (Oxford Publishing Co, 2nd edition, 2010)

An Illustrated History of the Snowdon Mountain Railway (Oxford Publishing Co, 2010)

Immortal Rails – the story of the closure and revival of the Ffestiniog Railway 1939-1983 (RailRomances, 2 volumes, 2004/5)

Macmillan, Nigel S. C. *The Campbeltown & Machrihanish Light Railway* (Plateway Press, 1993)

Milner, W. J. *Rails through the Sand* [Fairbourne Railway] (RailRomances, 1996)

Milner, John & Williams, Beryl *Rails to Glyn Ceiriog Part 1* [Glyn Valley Tramway] (Ceiriog Press, 2011)

Patterson, E. M. *The Ballycastle Railway* (Colourpoint Books, 2nd edition, 2006)

The Castlederg and Victoria Bridge Tramway (Colourpoint Books, 1998)

The Clogher Valley Railway (Colourpoint Books, 2nd edition, 2004)

The County Donegal Railways (David & Charles, 3rd edition, 1982)

The Lough Swilly Railway (David & Charles, revised edition, 1988)

The Mid-Antrim Narrow Gauge (Colourpoint Books, 2007)

Ransom, P. J. G. *Narrow Gauge Steam* (Oxford Publishing Co, 1996)

Rowlands, David, McGrath, Walter & Francis, Tom *The Dingle Train* (Plateway Press, 1996)

Shill, R. A. *Industrial Locomotives of West Midlands* (Industrial Railway Society, 1992)

Snell, J. B. *One Man's Railway* [Romney, Hythe & Dymchurch Railway] (David St John Thomas Publisher, 1993)

Spooner, C. E. *Narrow Gauge Railways* (E. & F. N. Spon, 1871)

Taylor, Alan R. & Tonks Eric S. *The Southwold Railway* (Ian Allan, 1979)

Taylor, Patrick *The West Clare Railway* (Plateway Press, 1994)

Thomas, Cliff *The Narrow Gauge in Britain & Ireland* (Atlantic Publishers, 2002)

Tonks, Eric *The Ironstone Quarries of the Midlands, Part V The Kettering Area* (Runpast Publishing, 1991)

The Ironstone Quarries of the Midlands, Part VII Rutland (Runpast Publishing, 1989)

The Ironstone Quarries of the Midlands, Part IX Leicestershire (Runpast Publishing, 1992)

Wade, E. A. *The Plynlimon & Hafan Tramway* (Twelveheads Press, 1997)

Waywell, Robin & Jux, Frank *Industrial Locomotives of the County of London* (Industrial Railway Society, 2008)

Index of Railways